THE
SECOND
WORLD WAR
IN 100 OBJECTS

THE STORY OF THE WORLD'S GREATEST CONFLICT TOLD THROUGH THE OBJECTS THAT SHAPED IT

MAJOR GENERAL
JULIAN THOMPSON CB OBE
AND
DR ALLAN R MILLETT
SENIOR MILITARY ADVISOR FOR THE
NATIONAL WORLD WAR II MUSEUM

ANDRE
DEUTSCH

THIS IS AN ANDRÉ DEUTSCH BOOK

This edition published in 2017 by André Deutsch
A division of the Carlton Publishing Group
20 Mortimer Street
London W1T 3JW

First published in 2012

10 9 8 7 6 5 4 3 2 1

Text © items 1–25, 27–29, 31–36, 38–40, 42–46, 48–49,
51–52, 54–57, 59–61, 63–72, 74–77, 79, 81–82,
84–86, 88–90, 92–94, 96 and 98–100 Julian Thompson 2012

Text © items 26, 30, 37, 41, 47, 50, 53, 58, 62, 73, 78, 80,
83, 87, 91, 95 and 97 Allan Millett 2012

Design © Carlton Books Limited 2012, 2017

A CIP catalogue record for this book is available from the British
Library.

ISBN 978 0 23300 524 9

Printed in Dubai

CONTENTS

1 Peace in Our Time 6

2 Führer Directive Number 1 10

3 The Yellow Star 12

4 The Enigma Machine 14

5 The SS Insignia 16

6 The Stuka 18

7 Winter Skis 20

8 The *Admiral Graf Spee* 24

9 Churchill's Cigar 26

10 The U-boat 28

11 The Maginot Line 30

12 Civilian Gas Masks 32

13 The Mitsubishi A6M Zero 34

14 The 88-mm Gun 36

15 The Little Ships 38

16 The Airborne Smock 42

17 The Cross of Lorraine 44

18 The Spitfire 48

19 The Messerschmitt Bf 109 50

20 The Fairey Swordfish 54

21 An Air Raid Shelter 56

22 HMS *Hood* 60

23 The Parachute X-Type 62

24 The Sten Gun 64

25 The T-34 Tank 66

26 The Atlantic Charter 70

27 An Air Raid Warden's Helmet 74

28 The Mosin-Nagant Rifle 76

29 The SAS Cap Insignia 78

30 The Boeing B-17 80

31 Oboe 84

32 The Human Torpedo 86

33 Japanese Headgear 90

34 The Secret Radio 92

35 A Silk Escape Map 94

36 The Bombe and Colossus 96

37 The *Stars and Stripes* 98

38 The Auster Light Aircraft 100

39 An MG 42 German Machine Gun 102

40 PLUTO 104

41 The Jeep 106

42 The Green Beret 108

43 The Panzerfaust 110

44 Montgomery's Beret and Tank 114

45 The Midget Submarine 116

46 The Avro Lancaster Bomber 120

47 US Airborne Divisional Insignia 122

48 The Desert Rats Insignia 126

49 Australian Divisional Badges 128

50 The USS *Enterprise* 130

51 The Long Range Desert Group Vehicle 134

52 The Commando Dagger 136

53 The Purple Heart 138

54 Canoes 140

55 Kamikaze 142

56 Penicillin 146

57 Depth Charge 148

58 C and K Rations 150

59 The Bridge over the River Kwai 152

60 CAM Ships 154

61 The Atlantic Wall 156

62 Liberty Ships 158

63 The Bouncing Bomb 160

64 Ration Books 164

65 The Owen Gun 166

66 The Chindit Insignia 170

67 ASDIC 172

68 Beach Defences 174

69 The Nebelwerfer 178

70 The WACO Glider 180

71 The LST 182

72 The George Cross 184

73 The Rocket Launcher 186

74 The Tunnellers' Trolley 188

75 Eisenhower's Unsent Message 190

76 The Tiger Tank 192

77 Popski's Private Army Insignia 194

78 Blood Plasma 196

79 The Bailey Bridge 198

80 The DUKW 200

81 The Bangalore Torpedo 202

82 The Tallboy Bomb 204

83 The Grumman F6F Hellcat 206

84 The DD Tank 208

85 A German Prison-Camp Watchtower 210

86 Hobart's Funnies 212

87 The M-1 Rifle 214

88 A Mulberry Harbour 216

89 The German Half-Track Armoured Vehicle 218

90 The French First Army Insignia 220

91 The Sherman Tank 224

92 The Victoria Cross 226

93 The Goliath German Mini-Tank 228

94 A Parachute Supply Container 230

95 Canadian Army Insignia 232

96 The *Volkssturm* Armband 236

97 The P-51 Mustang 240

98 V-Weapons 242

99 Hitler's Eagle's Nest and the Berghof 246

100 The Atomic Bomb 250

INTRODUCTION

The 100 objects in this book all have a vital connection with the Second World War. Some were conceived before that war, and others during it, but all formed an essential part of the "tapestry" of that conflict. My aim in this book was to produce pictures and text that would resonate with readers whether they were experts on the Second World War or approaching the subject for the first time. I chose objects only, not people. My choice ranges from the biggest object, the Atlantic Wall, to an ampoule of penicillin. Among the big objects, I include the Maginot Line, the two Mulberry Harbours and the Bridge over the River Kwai, or to give it its proper name at the time; the Mae Klong. The smaller objects include Churchill's cigar and insignias for the SAS, Popski's Private Army, the SS and the Desert Rats, as well as Australian divisional patches.

I wanted to include objects associated with the Germans, Japanese and Italians, as well as British, American, Russian, French, Australian and other Allied nations who used some of the same equipment. Three of the most famous tanks of the war appear here: the Russian T-34, the German Tiger and American Sherman; this last used extensively by the British as well. The Italians were the first to use human torpedoes to attack ships; other nations quickly followed suit, and their torpedoes appear in the book as well. Numerous vehicles became famous in the Second World War, none more so than the ubiquitous Jeep, though the amphibious DUKW (Duck) was probably a close second. Arguably the most deadly anti-tank gun of the Second World War, the German 88-mm appears in both its guises: anti-tank and anti-aircraft.

Several documents appear in the book. Right at the beginning is the piece of paper that Neville Chamberlain waved for the crowd to see when he returned to London from meeting Adolf Hitler in Munich, telling them that this guaranteed "Peace in our time". Just 11 months later, Hitler issued his first war directive ordering the invasion of Poland and the Second World War had begun. The third document, created by President Roosevelt and Prime Minister Churchill on board HMS *Prince of Wales* at Placentia Bay Newfoundland in August 1941, became adapted as the Charter of the United Nations – which is also reproduced here. The final document did not see the light of day until a month after it was written: a note penned by General Eisenhower to be used in the event of the 6 June 1944 Normandy landings failing.

As well as the Spitfire, among the other aircraft depicted in the book the famous "Flying Fortress" B-17 bomber, the Mustang, the BF109 Messerschmitt and the Zero all appear, along with the "String bag" Swordfish and the Lancaster bomber. The carrier USS *Enterprise* (the celebrated "Big E") is here, along with HMS *Hood*, the *Graf Spee* and the "little ships" of Dunkirk.

I hope that readers will enjoy reading about the chosen items in *The Second World War in 100 objects*, and find the book both informative and perhaps that it throws a light on some generally less well known facts.

Julian Thompson

ABOVE: One of the most iconic items of the Second World War, the British Mark III combat helmet.

◼ Peace in Our Time

On the afternoon of 30 September 1938, the Prime Minister of the United Kingdom, Neville Chamberlain, left Munich in a British Airways Super Lockheed Electra and landed at Heston airport, near today's Heathrow. A huge crowd greeted him. Facing a battery of microphones, he waved a piece of paper, saying, "This morning I had another talk with the German Chancellor, Herr Hitler, and here is a paper which bears his name as well as mine." The police cleared a route through the mob to enable him to drive to Buckingham Palace, where he appeared on the balcony with the King and Queen. That evening, he addressed a crowd from an upper window in Downing Street: "My good friends, this is the second time in our history that there has come back from Germany to Downing Street peace with honour. I believe it is peace in our time."

Chamberlain's visit to Munich was his third trip to see Hitler in 15 days as a result of a crisis concerning Czechoslovakia. In 1938 Czechoslovakia's total population of around 14 million included some three million German speakers, most whom lived in an area known as Sudetenland. In early September, the Sudetenlanders, stoked by Hitler's inflammatory speeches and with strong Nazi support, rioted, demanding union with Germany. By 15 September the Czech authorities had restored order, but there was an atmosphere of mounting tension across Europe.

That day, Chamberlain flew to the Berghof, Berchtesgaden, to persuade Hitler not to invade Czechoslovakia. He proposed that where more than half of the population desired union with Germany they should be granted their wish, to which Hitler agreed. The French reluctantly joined the British in putting pressure on President Beneš of Czechoslovakia to agree. Chamberlain returned to London, but Hitler, in a classic blackmailer's ploy, said the concessions were insufficient.

On 22 September, Chamberlain flew to meet Hitler at the Dreesen Hotel in Bad Godesberg, one of Hitler's favourite watering holes. Chamberlain was inclined to concede to Hitler's demands, but was opposed by his own Cabinet. On 23 September the Czechs mobilized and the British Royal Navy was deployed to war stations. Britain prepared for war. Chamberlain broadcast on 27 September: "How horrible, fantastic, incredible it is that we should be digging trenches and trying on gas-masks here because of a quarrel in a faraway country between people of whom we know nothing."

An appeal to Benito Mussolini, First Marshal of the Empire of Italy, to mediate signalled to Hitler that the French and British would crumble. On 29 September, Chamberlain flew to Munich along with Édouard Daladier, the French Prime Minister. They met Hitler and Mussolini at the Führerbau, the new neoclassical Nazi party headquarters. Here they accepted terms put forward by Mussolini but drafted by the German Foreign Office, conceding virtually all Hitler's demands. The next morning Chamberlain met Hitler in his private apartment, for what the former described as "a very friendly and pleasant talk", during which they signed the paper that Chamberlain showed at Heston.

German troops occupied Sudetenland immediately. They delayed occupying the rest of Czechoslovakia until May 1939, Hitler declaring, "I shall not occupy Prague for six months or so. I can't bring myself to do such a thing to the old fellow at the moment."

Strategic experts still disagree over whether the year's delay before the outbreak of the Second World War benefitted Germany or the Allies. Perhaps Chamberlain's climbdown caused Hitler to underestimate the British, to his ultimate cost. In August 1939 he said to his generals, "Our enemies are small worms. I saw them at Munich."

We, the German Führer and Chancellor and the British Prime Minister, have had a further meeting today and are agreed in recognising that the question of Anglo-German relations is of the first importance for the two countries and for Europe.

We regard the agreement signed last night and the Anglo-German Naval Agreement as symbolic of the desire of our two peoples never to go to war with one another again.

We are resolved that the method of consultation shall be the method adopted to deal with any other questions that may concern our two countries, and we are determined to continue our efforts to remove possible sources of difference and thus to contribute to assure the peace of Europe.

Neville Chamberlain

September 30. 1938.

LEFT: Chamberlain at Heston airport on 30 September 1938 on his return from Munich.

ABOVE: The paper with Hitler's and Chamberlain's signature.

OVERLEAF: Chamberlain greeted by an SS guard of honour on his arrival at Munich. The German foreign minister von Ribbentrop is on Chamberlain's left.

2 Führer Directive Number 1

From the moment Adolf Hitler became Chancellor of Germany in January 1933, he had directed the country's armed forces with political aims, ordering a programme of rearmament in direct violation of the terms of the Treaty of Versailles (1920) and readying the military for a series of aggressive actions aimed at constructing a Greater German Reich. His direction of (and interference in) military affairs was characterized by a series of directives to the army. More general and forward-looking than simple orders, these *Führerdirektivs* tended to be of a strategic nature, beginning in autumn 1933 with the "Directive for the Armed Forces in the Event of Sanctions" and continuing in March 1938 with a "Directive 1" which ordered the Anschluss that annexed Austria. To enable his will to be transmitted throughout the armed forces with a minimum of political interference or modification by the traditional military hierarchy, on 4 February 1938 Hitler replaced the old Defence Ministry with the OKW (*Oberkommando der Wehrmacht*, High Command of the Armed Forces) headed up by one of his own placemen, General Wilhelm Keitel (an officer so unpopular with operational officers for his slavish subservience to Hitler's will that he became known as *Lakeitel*, "lackey").

Plans for the projected assault on Poland (known as "Case White") were first circulated on 3 April 1939, but the assault was delayed until the autumn to give time to isolate the country diplomatically and to broker the agreement with the Soviet Union on Poland's dismemberment which bore fruit with the Nazi-Soviet Pact of 24 August.

By the fourth week in August, all was ready; Hitler gambled that France and Britain would lack the political will to intervene on behalf of Poland, and this is reflected in the first of a new series of *Führerdirektivs*. Directive Number 1, dated 31 August 1939, self-servingly summarized the scenario in its opening words: "Since the situation on Germany's eastern frontier has become intolerable and all political possibilities of peaceful settlement have been exhausted, I have decided upon a solution by force." A brief invocation of Case White as the template for the coming operation against Poland is followed by a much longer section concerned with the West. Germany's armed forces are ordered at all costs to respect the neutrality of Holland, Belgium, Luxembourg and Switzerland and warned that the blame for hostilities opening in western Europe must be laid firmly at the door of Britain and France. Whenever, however, either of those two countries might engage in aggressive moves against Germany, then the neutrality of the others could be violated with impunity in order to outflank the French defensive positions.

The declarations of war by Britain and France against Germany on 3 September provided Hitler with this pretext, leading to the issue of *Führerdirectiv* 2 ("For the Conduct of the War") the same day. The series continued until Directive 51 (of 3 November 1943), which gave orders for the disposition of the army to fight against the Allied opening of a second front in the West. Long before this, the style of the directives had turned from strategic judgments to Hitler's more typical micromanaging of operational military matters, which undercut operational officers' authority and undermined any rational direction of the war effort. From November 1943, with the war turning defensive, Hitler abandoned the *Führerdirektiv* format in favour of a series of ad hoc *Führer* orders and orders of the day, a stream which only finally ceased on 15 April (1945), just a fortnight before his suicide, with a last, hopeless call for resistance against the "Bolshevik" onslaught.

ABOVE: The German invasion of Poland, 1 September 1939.

RIGHT: Hitler's Directive Number 1, issued on 31 August 1939, ordered the invasion of Poland.

C-126c

Der Oberste Befehlshaber der Wehrmacht   Berlin, den   39.
OKW/WFA Nr. 170 /39 g.K.Chefs. L I

8 Ausfertigungen
2. Ausfertigung.

Weisung Nr. 1
für die Kriegführung.

1.) Nachdem alle politischen Möglichkeiten erschöpft sind, um
auf friedlichem Wege eine für Deutschland unerträgliche Lage
an seiner Ostgrenze zu beseitigen, habe ich mich zur
gewaltsamen Lösung entschlossen.

2.) Der Angriff gegen Polen ist nach den für Fall Weiss getrof-
fenen Vorbereitungen zu führen mit den Abänderungen, die
sich beim Heer durch den inzwischen fast vollendeten Auf-
marsch ergeben.

Aufgabenverteilung und Operationsziel bleiben unver-
ändert.

Angriffstag: .1.9.39..

Angriffszeit ....

Diese Zeit gilt auch für die Unternehmungen Gdingen -
Danziger Bucht und Brücke Dirschau.

3.) Im Westen kommt es darauf an, die Verantwortung für die Er-
öffnung von Feindseligkeiten eindeutig England und Frankreich zu überlassen. Geringfügigen Grenzverletzungen ist
zunächst rein örtlich entgegen zu treten.

Die von uns Holland, Belgien, Luxemburg und der
Schweiz zugesicherte Neutralität ist peinlich zu achten.

- 2 -

- 2 -

Die deutsche Westgrenze ist zu Lande an keiner Stelle
ohne meine ausdrückliche Genehmigung zu überschreiten.

Zur See gilt das gleiche für alle kriegerischen oder
als solche zu deutenden Handlungen.

Die defensiven Massnahmen der Luftwaffe sind zunächst auf die unbedingte Abwehr feindl. Luftangriffe an
der Reichsgrenze zu beschränken, wobei so lange als mög-
lich die Grenze der neutralen Staaten bei der Abwehr ein-
zelner Flugzeuge und kleinerer Einheiten zu achten ist.
Erst wenn beim Einsatz stärkerer franz. und engl. Angriffs-
verbände über die neutralen Staaten gegen deutsches Gebiet die Luftverteidigung im Westen nicht mehr gesichert
ist, ist die Abwehr auch über diesem neutralen Gebiet frei-
zugeben.

Schnellste Orientierung des OKW über jede Verletzung
der Neutralität dritter Staaten durch die Westgegner ist
besonders wichtig.

4.) Eröffnen England und Frankreich die Feindseligkeiten
gegen Deutschland, so ist es Aufgabe der im Westen ope-
rierenden Teile der Wehrmacht, unter möglichster Schonung
der Kräfte die Voraussetzungen für den siegreichen Ab-
schluss der Operationen gegen Polen zu erhalten. Im Rahmen
dieser Aufgabe sind die feindl. Streitkräfte und de-
ren wehrwirtschaftl. Kraftquellen nach Kräften zu schädi-
gen. Den Befehl zum Beginn von Angriffshandlungen behalte
ich mir in jedem Fall vor.

- 3 -

- 3 -

Das Heer hält den Westwall und trifft Vorbereitungen, dessen Umfassung im Norden - unter Verletzung belg.
oder holländ. Gebietes durch die Westmächte - zu verhindern. Rücken franz. Kräfte in Luxemburg ein, so bleibt
die Sprengung der Grenzbrücken freigegeben.

Die Kriegsmarine führt Handelskrieg mit dem Schwer-
punkt gegen England. Zur Verstärkung der Wirkung kann
mit der Erklärung von Gefahrenzonen gerechnet werden.
OKM meldet, in welchen Seegebieten und in welchem Umfang
Gefahrenzonen für zweckmässig gehalten werden. Der Wort-
laut für eine öffentl. Erklärung ist im Benehmen mit dem
Ausw. Amte vorzubereiten und mir über OKW zur Genehmigung vorzulegen.

Die Ostsee ist gegen feindl. Einbruch zu sichern.
Die Entscheidung, ob zu diesem Zwecke die Ostsee-Eingänge
mit Minen gesperrt werden dürfen, trifft Ob.d.M.
bleibt vorbehalten.

Die Luftwaffe hat in erster Linie den Einsatz der
franz. und engl. Luftwaffe gegen das deutsche Heer und
den deutschen Lebensraum zu verhindern.

Bei der Kampfführung gegen England ist der Einsatz
der Luftwaffe zur Störung der engl. Seezufuhr, der
Rüstungsindustrie, der Truppentransporte nach Frankreich
vorzubereiten. Günstige Gelegenheit zu einem wirkungs-
vollen Angriff gegen massierte engl. Flotteneinheiten,
insbes. gegen Schlachtschiffe und Flugzeugträger ist aus-

- 4 -

- 4 -

zunutzen. Angriffe gegen London bleiben meiner Entscheidung vorbehalten.

Die Angriffe gegen das engl. Mutterland sind unter
dem Gesichtspunkt vorzubereiten, dass unzureichender Er-
folg mit Teilkräften unter allen Umständen zu vermeiden
ist.

Verteiler:

OKH	1. Ausf.
OKM	2. "
R.d.L.u.Ob.d.L.	3. "
OKW:	
Chef WFA	4. "
L	5.-8. "

▪3 The Yellow Star

The yellow six-pointed Star of David with the word "*Jude*" (Jew) is universally known as a badge worn by Jews as part of their victimization by the Nazis. Although the persecution of Jews in Germany began as soon as Hitler came to power in 1933, they were not required to wear a badge or other sign marking them out from the rest of society. But yellow stars of David were painted on the windows of Jewish-owned shops as early as 1 April 1933, the date on which the Nazis declared a boycott on these premises. This offensive graffiti does not appear to have been officially organized, because the matter of special Jewish badges had not yet been a subject for discussion among Nazi leaders. More likely, ordinary rank-and-file Nazi party members and probably the SA (*Sturmabteilung* or Stormtroopers) recipitated the paint-daubing ploy and the idea caught on, spreading quickly around Germany thanks to the media, especially the radio.

On 7 November 1938, Ernst vom Rath, Third Secretary at the German Embassy in Paris, was assassinated by Herschel Grynszpan, a Polish Jew. In retaliation, Reinhard Heydrich, Chief of the Sicherheitsdienst – Security Service (SD) – ordered the destruction of all places of Jewish worship in Germany and Austria. This action had long been prepared; the murder of vom Rath merely provided the excuse to begin the atrocity on the night of 9 November. As well as demolishing 177 synagogues, bands of Nazi hooligans destroyed an estimated 7,500 Jewish shops. Streets in every town were covered in broken glass, and the event was named *Kristallnacht* (Crystal Night, or Night of Broken Glass). On 12 November, at a meeting of Nazi leaders, Heydrich suggested a special badge for Jews. But no action was taken for nearly a year.

It was not until after the defeat of Poland in September 1939 that Jewish badges were introduced in the German-occupied sector (the Soviet Union occupied the eastern part of Poland). To begin with, there was no laid-down policy, and it was left to individual Nazi officials whether to issue orders that Jews in their area of jurisdiction were to wear badges. The designs varied from place to place. However, on 23 November 1939, Hans Frank, the German Governor General of Occupied Poland, ordered that all Jews above the age of ten were to wear a white armband with a yellow Star of David on their right arm. By December 1942, more than 85 per cent of the Jewish people in Poland had been transported to extermination camps. This figure included Jews living in the former Soviet Polish territory, as by now the Russians had been pushed out following Hitler's invasion of Russia in June 1941.

An instruction published on 1 September 1941 had ordered all Jews in Germany and Poland to wear the yellow Star of David with "*Jude*" inscribed on it, on the left side of the chest. This order was then extended to include Jews in most occupied territories and countries. There is a legend that when Jews in Denmark were ordered to wear the star, King Christian X wore one and his example was followed by the whole population, Jew and Gentile, causing the Germans to rescind the order. In fact, the Germans never required Danish Jews to wear the star. What is not legend is the reaction by the Danes to discovering that 7,500 Danish Jews were about to be deported to death camps. Most of these Jews were hidden by their neighbours, and many were subsequently smuggled out to Sweden.

LEFT: French Jews after being rounded up in Paris and held in a covered cycling stadium, photographed in a transit camp, at Drancy north east of Paris in July 1942. From here they were taken by train to extermination camps in the east.

ABOVE: The yellow Star of David.

■4 The Enigma Machine

Enigma is the codeword for a cipher machine based on a design by Dutchman, H A Koch. His ideas were developed by a Berlin engineer, Dr Arthur Scherbius, who first marketed it in 1923. By 1929 both the German army and navy had purchased different versions of it. Later it was bought by the Luftwaffe, the SS (*Schutzstaffel* or Protection Squadron), the *Abwehr* (the German secret service) and the *Reichsbahn* (German state railways). The machine consisted of a set of three rotating discs, called rotors, connected to a keyboard and a series of electrically powered lights. When a key was pressed the rotor would turn, and a display lamp would illuminate a letter.

To encrypt a message, the operator would press the alphabetical key for the initial letter of the message, for example B, and the X lamp might light up. In earlier versions of Enigma, the operator copied down the resulting series of letters on to a message pad. Eventually the message would consist of an apparently meaningless jumble of letters, which in turn were transmitted by radio. The enigma operator at the receiving end would adjust his machine to the settings of the day and decrypt the message in the same way.

Throughout the Second World War, the Germans believed that the Enigma was unbreakable because for every signal sent there were millions of possible solutions. Every day the rotor settings were changed, and possessing a machine was only part way to breaking the code; you had

to know what the day's setting was. The limitations to Enigma were that there are only 26 letters in the alphabet, that no letter could stand for itself, and that there were no numeral keys, so figures had to be spelled out.

The Poles acquired an Enigma machine and started reading some German signal traffic as early as 1932. They passed on the information to the French in 1939, and the British in 1940. The British Government Code and Cypher School at Bletchley Park began to break the Luftwaffe Enigma codes during the Norwegian and French campaigns of 1940, but took longer to read the German navy traffic. During the Battle of Britain (10 July–31 October 1940), most Luftwaffe traffic was sent over landlines, and consequently could not be read by Bletchley Park. The gravest crisis for the Allies arose during the Battle of the Atlantic when Admiral Dönitz's U-boat command began to use a fourth rotor on their Enigma machines, hugely multiplying the complexity of the enciphering of messages. The new German system was codenamed "Shark". Brilliant work by Bletchley Park eventually resulted in the deciphering of much of the U-boat command signals, and eventually the breaking of "Shark", assisted by the fact that Dönitz controlled his U-boats so precisely that he transmitted a huge volume of radio traffic, believing "Shark" to be unbreakable.

A number of Enigma machines were captured during the Second World War, but these only provided a partial

OPPOSITE: General Heinz Guderian commanding XIX Panzer Corps in his command half-track during the Battle of France 1940 with an Enigma Machine.

RIGHT: A three-ring Enigma cypher machine in wooden transit case, circa1930s.

breakthrough in reading German signal traffic. In March 1941, during a Commando raid on the Lofoten Islands off Norway, the German trawler *Krebs* was taken, with two Enigma machines and the current settings. In May 1941 and July 1941, the British captured two German weather ships, acquiring their codebooks for the following months. In May 1941, U-110 was forced to the surface, and sailors from HMS *Bulldog* boarded and seized her

Enigma machine and codes before she sank. In October 1942, HMS *Petard* depth-charged U-559 to the surface and captured the latest codebooks. In June 1944, sailors from the USS *Pittsburgh* boarded the surfaced U-505, capturing her codebooks.

The work of Bletchley Park in breaking the German cyphers was greatly assisted by the invention of the "Bombe", an early form of computer.

■5 The SS Insignia

Although there were a multiplicity of SS badges depending on the type of uniform worn and the unit, two themes were common: the double lightning flash and the death's head. The SS, short for *Schutzstaffel*, literally meaning "defence echelon", began its existence as the black-shirted personal guard for Hitler. Heinrich Himmler, a chicken farmer by trade who had never served as a soldier or heard a shot fired in action, was appointed by Hitler to command this guard. It was formed from the SA, the brown-shirt storm troopers of the Nazi party who had played a leading part in bringing Hitler to power. From small beginnings the SS was expanded into a very large force, an alternative army, whose main task in Himmler's eyes was to ensure the continuing existence of Nazi power.

The name *Schutzstaffel* was abbreviated to SS, depicted as a double lightning flash in imitation of ancient runic characters. This double flash was worn on a black collar patch, often just on one side of the collar. Although it became the insignia for all SS units, at first it was confined to members of Hitler's guard, the *Leibstandarte* Adolf Hitler,

which after Hitler's accession to power moved from Munich to take over bodyguard duties from the Army Chancellery Guard in Berlin.

The other badge worn by the SS, usually on the front of their caps below the German eagle, was the death's head, the *Totenkopf*. This, with their black uniforms, was a copy of the outfit and headdress worn by the Life Guard Cavalry of the Prussian kings and German emperors, the "Death's Head" Hussars or *Leibhusaren*. In addition to collar and cap badges, the SS took to wearing cuff bands to denote their unit: the *Leibstandarte* Adolf Hitler wore one embroidered Adolf Hitler; the 2nd SS Panzer Division (*Das Reich*) wore a *Das Reich* cuff band, and so on.

From its original strength of 117 men, the Leibstandarte soon expanded into two battalions commanded by Sepp Dietrich, Hitler's personal bodyguard and chauffeur. On

30 June 1934 the Liebstandarte took part in the night of the "Long Knives" when Hitler ordered the elimination of Ernst Röhm, the Chief of Staff of the SA. The executioners led by Dietrich, and several Liebstandarte NCOs (non-commissioned officers) including the Drum Major killed six SA men in Munich, and three in Berlin. One of the motives behind these murders was an unspoken agreement between Hitler and the army that the SA would not become a rival army. The SA did not, but the SS most certainly did.

During 1934–35 more SS units were formed into SS-*Verfugüngtruppe* (SS-VT), or Special Purpose Troops, including two new *Standarten* (regiments), the Germania and the Deutschland. A motorized battalion of the *Leibstandarte* led the German occupation force into Austria in March 1938. In July 1938, Hitler announced that all SS-VT *Standarten* would form part of the army in war. By 1943, the *Leibstandarte* had become the 1st SS Panzer Division *Leibstandarte*, and the *Deutschland* and *Der Führer* the 2nd SS Panzer Division *Das Reich*. Eventually there were almost a quarter of a million SS troops in 38 divisions of the Waffen SS, as the SS-VT came to be called. So much for Hitler's promise to the army. The Waffen SS acquired a reputation as fanatical and highly competent soldiers in the Second World War, but this should not obscure the fact that they carried out numerous atrocities against both soldiers and civilians, notably in Russia and France. The SS even had a slang word for it, *rabatz*, meaning "having fun killing everyone in sight".

Even more notorious for their atrocities were the concentration-camp guard units, the SS-*Totenkopfverbände* (SS-TV), a separate part of the SS from the Waffen although they did provide the manpower for the 3rd SS Panzer Division Totenkopf. Unlike the Waffen, the SS-TV wore a death's head insignia on their tunics. Under the direction of the murderous ex-chicken-farmer Himmler, they enslaved and murdered millions.

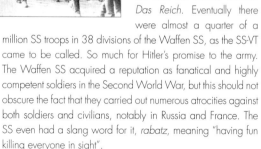

LEFT: The Nuremburg Rally 1933. The motto on the standards is
"Deutschland Erwache" (Germany Awake).

ABOVE: An SS insignia in bronze, with silver-plated runes.

17

◼6 The Stuka

The Stuka Junkers 87 bomber was designed to provide close support for the German army. It was inspired by the experience of the First World War when, by 1918, the German army was on the receiving end of fire delivered by the Royal Flying Corps and later the RAF in support of the British Army. The Germans further developed the techniques for this tactic, in stark contrast to the British. By 1939, the RAF was paying lip service to close air support of ground forces in the interests of pursuing an independent war strategy which disregarded the needs of the other two services. The German tactical doctrine of pushing their armour far ahead carried with it the risk that the tanks would outrun their artillery support. Tactical air support would fill the gap, especially the Stuka dive-bomber.

The Stuka's dive-bombing attack was especially effective in towns, and against vehicles on roads, when these were all lined up like ducks in a row. It was not so effective against infantry well spread out in open country, but it took a long time for troops to realize this. The psychological terror effect was enhanced by a wind-driven siren mounted on the fixed undercarriage which gave out a loud wailing scream as it dived. The technique used by the Stuka pilots was to put the aircraft into a steep dive from about 1,800 metres (6,000 feet), aiming the aircraft at the target using his ailerons to keep it aligned, while the dive brakes automatically kept the dive at the correct angle. As soon as the bombs were released, usually at about 275 metres (900 feet), an automatic recovery system pulled the Stuka out of its near-vertical dive. The G-force on the aircrew was around force six. Stukas often dropped their bombs within a few metres of the target, and even achieved direct hits. This was something a conventional bomber could only achieve by sheer luck.

The Stuka was fitted with a twin-barrelled rear-firing twin machine gun but, with a fixed undercarriage and gull wings, the aircraft was slow, and its rear gun gave little protection against well-flown modern fighters. The Stuka was especially vulnerable during the pull-up from its dive. The Spitfires and Hurricanes created such mayhem among the Stukas when they took part in the Battle of Britain that they were withdrawn from that particular contest.

The Stuka was used to great effect in Russia and in North Africa, in the role for which it was intended, destroying a significant number of tanks. The Stuka's successful time in North Africa came to an end when the RAF regained air superiority in early-to-mid-1942.

The Stuka also had a very long run of success at sea, especially in the Mediterranean, operating from airfields in Italy, the Greek Islands and the North African coast. This was partially the result of the fact that the Royal Navy did not have a really effective carrier-borne fighter until it acquired American Grumman Hellcats in 1944. That in turn was because aircraft procurement for the Royal Navy in the interwar years was in the hands of the RAF, resulting in a run of poor-performance aircraft ordered by a service that had no interest in carrier warfare – unlike the situation prevailing in the US and Japan.

Stukas inflicted heavy casualties, ship losses and damage to British convoys transiting the Mediterranean, especially those supplying Malta. They were also responsible for much damage in Malta itself, as well as to ships in the dockyard there, notably the carrier HMS *Illustrious*, in for repair. Stukas were used extensively in Crete in 1941, both in support of the German airborne landings and against ships evacuating the British troops when the island fell.

LEFT: Stukas over Stalingrad during the German assault on the city, September–October 1942.

ABOVE TOP: A Stuka (JU-87) starts a half-roll before a nosedive.

ABOVE BOTTOM: The Stuka was at its best in close support of ground troops, and in the anti-ship role, especially in the first half of the war, before the Allies gained air superiority.

▪ 7 Winter Skis

The Soviet Union invaded Finland on 30 November 1939 after the Finns refused to agree to territorial concessions demanded by the Russians in order to strengthen the defences of the Leningrad Military District. The Finnish Army consisted of ten divisions, which were short of many items of equipment, from artillery, mortars and radios to shells, but they were determined to defend Finnish independence, which had been gained from Russia after the Bolshevik revolution in 1917. The soldiers were well trained to use their initiative, and were at home in the forested terrain in both summer and winter. They could use their skis for mobility in snow, for example.

The Finns used the period of negotiations leading up to the Russian invasion to move to their defensive positions. Much of the 1,000-kilometre (620-mile) frontier was a trackless snow-covered wilderness of forests and lakes, impassable to a modern army. This allowed the Finnish commander, Carl Gustaf Emil Marshal Mannerheim, to concentrate six divisions along the 65-kilometre (40-mile) Mannerheim Line in the Karelian isthmus between Lake Lagoda and the Gulf of Finland, and another two on the 80 kilometres (50 miles) of Finnish frontier northeast of Lake Lagoda.

The Soviet Army deployed 26 divisions against Finland, comprising 1,200,000 men, with motor transport, plenty of artillery, 1,500 tanks and 3,000 aircraft. But it was a gravely flawed force, for Stalin's recent purges had stripped his army of good senior generals. Formation commanders were mainly sycophants terrified of their Communist Party apparatchik "political advisers" (ie minders). Soviet commanders were paralysed by indecision, fearing instant execution or, if they were lucky, the Gulag, should they demonstrate any initiative that departed from

Soviet military doctrine. The solders were amazingly ill prepared for winter warfare. They had no white camouflage clothing, inadequate frost protection for vehicles and equipment, and no ski troops – crushing disadvantages in a campaign fought in sub-arctic weather.

A Soviet attack by one division at Petsamo in the north was halted in its tracks. Amphibious assaults at Helsinki, Hanko and Turku on the southern coast were repelled. The main Russian thrust through the Karelian isthmus with 12 divisions supported by armour resulted in stalemate, with heavy Russian losses. Initially the Finns, who had no experience of armoured warfare and no anti-tank weapons, were disheartened by Soviet tanks, but they quickly learned that these could be hunted down in the long winter nights using "Molotov cocktails", especially as Russian armour operated without infantry support.

In late December, the Finns counterattacked along the eastern front, where they outflanked Soviet road-bound formations by using ski troops moving through the forests. The Soviet reaction was to form isolated "hedgehog" positions which, although well defended, were small and could be picked off one by one. At Suomussalmi between 11 December 1939 and 8 January 1940, two Soviet divisions, outnumbering the Finns by four or five to one, were strung out along miles of track. They were too cumbersome to react to the slashing attacks by Finnish ski troops who cut the Russians to pieces. The Finns captured 65 tanks, 437 trucks, 10 motorcycles, 92 field guns, 78 anti-tank guns, 13 anti-aircraft guns, 6,000 rifles, 290 machine guns and large numbers of radios. It cost in addition 27,500 Soviet dead, 43 knocked-out tanks and 270 other vehicles destroyed. The Finns lost 900 dead and 1,770 wounded. On 1 February 1940, a reorganized Soviet Army under General Semyon

LEFT: Finnish soldier advancing with rifle at the ready, ski poles tucked under his arm.

ABOVE: Finns carrying out stem turns as they descend. The Finnish skill on cross-country skis made them far more mobile than their opponent infantry.

OVERLEAF: A posed picture of Finnish infantry in gas masks and white camouflage.

Timoshenko, reinforced by nine fresh divisions, bludgeoned the Finnish defences with a series of mass attacks, regardless of Russian casualties. On 13 February the Red Army broke through at Summa, and began to roll up the Finnish defences. On 12 March, the Finns agreed to peace terms.

The Soviet Union lost 200,000 dead and much equipment. Finland lost 25,000 dead and one-tenth of its territory. One of the major consequences of Soviet ineptitude in what became known as the "Winter War" was that Britain, the USA and especially Germany greatly underrated Russian military potential. In June 1941, at the start of Operation Barbarossa, Hitler thought that Russia would be a pushover. For several months after he invaded Russia, the British and Americans tended to share this view.

■8 The *Admiral Graf Spee*

The "pocket battleship" *Admiral Graf Spee* was the last of three *Deutschland* class cruisers, laid down before Adolf Hitler came to power, while Germany still observed the terms of the Versailles Treaty of 1919. This treaty allowed Germany to build warships with a maximum displacement of 10,000 tons. In fact the class exceeded the displacement by 1,700 tons.

The *Admiral Graf Spee* and its sisters (*Deutschland* and *Admiral Scheer*) were not battleships, but heavily armed, thinly protected, long-range merchant raiders, stronger than any faster ship, and also faster than any other stronger vessels, except for the British battle cruisers *Hood*, *Renown* and *Repulse*. They were potentially a very serious threat. If the Germans had built all eight of the class, as permitted by the Treaty, three British battle cruisers would have been insufficient to match them – and the Washington Naval Treaty (6 February 1922) did not allow Britain to build any more battle cruisers.

On 21 and 23 August 1939, while diplomatic moves were being made to resolve the crisis over Danzig that eventually led to the outbreak of the Second World War, the *Admiral Graf Spee* and the *Deutschland* sailed from Wilhelmshaven for their intended areas of operations – the *Graf Spee* to the South Atlantic and the *Deutschland* to the North Atlantic. Their purpose: to strain British sea power by posing a constant threat to merchant-shipping routes. There were plenty of targets, because an average of 2,500 ships flying the Red Ensign were at sea on any given day. The two pocket battleships were permitted by Hitler to commence operations on 24 September, following the failure of his "peace initiative" after he had crushed Poland.

The *Deutschland* sank only two merchantmen before being recalled to Germany and renamed *Lützow*; it would never do if the "Germany" were to be sunk. Eventually, after the *Graf Spee* under Captain Langsdorff had sunk nine ships, Commodore Harwood with the heavy cruiser *Exeter* and light cruisers *Ajax* and *Achilles* located her 240 kilometres (150 miles) off the River Plate estuary in Uruguay, on 12 December 1939.

The *Graf Spee* was more heavily armoured than the *Exeter*, and with six 28-cm (11-in) guns in two triple turrets, and secondary armament of eight 15-cm (5.9-in) guns, outgunned the heavy cruiser, let alone the light cruisers with their 15.2-cm (6-in) guns. *Graf Spee* had 54,000-horsepower diesel engines which gave her a radius of action of 16,000 kilometres (10,000 miles) at cruising, even without refuelling from her attendant supply ship – more than twice the radius of a steam-turbine ship. She had a catapult-launched seaplane and search radar to scan the sea for victims or enemy warships. At this time very few British ships were fitted with radar.

Notwithstanding the disparity in size and gun power, Commodore Harwood ordered his ships to engage *Graf Spee* on two sides. A running battle ensued, with *Graf Spee* in Harwood's words "wriggling like an eel behind smoke screens". His fire was very accurate. *Exeter* was so badly damaged she had to retire, but the two light cruisers kept

LEFT: The *Admiral Graf Spee* after being scuttled on the orders of her captain.

ABOVE: The "pocket battleship" *Admiral Graf Spee* off Montevideo with some of her crew over the side inspecting damage after the Battle of the River Plate.

up the fire. Soon they too were so damaged that Harwood ordered them to disengage. Instead of turning to crush the two light cruisers, Langsdorff kept heading for Montevideo in Uruguay. Admittedly he had suffered two flesh wounds and been temporarily knocked unconscious. Once in Montevideo, a clever deception scheme by the British persuaded Langsdorff that a large force had now assembled and was waiting for him to emerge. The plan included the British Ambassador in Montevideo making considerable efforts to delay the *Graf Spee*'s sailing, to gain time for British reinforcements to arrive in the shape of the carrier *Ark Royal* and the battle cruiser *Renown*.

Langsdorff came to the conclusion that to engage in battle would lead to the certain loss of his ship and pointless sacrifice of his crew. Admiral Raeder, the Commander-in-Chief (C-in-C) of

the German Navy, and Hitler both agreed that it was out of the question to accept internment of the *Graf Spee* by Uruguay.

At 16.15 hours on 17 December, the *Graf Spee* with a skeleton crew weighed anchor and moved slowly into the estuary of the Plate. At 7.36 pm, her ensign was hauled down. Twenty minutes later her structure was shattered by explosive charges. Amid billowing smoke and flames, she settled on a sandbank. The *Ark Royal* and *Renown* were still 1,600 kilometres (1,000 miles) away.

Three days later, Langsdorff wrapped himself up in the Imperial German Ensign (not the Swastika) and shot himself, having written in a final letter: "I alone bear the responsibility for scuttling the Panzerschiff *Admiral Graf Spee*. I am happy to pay with my life to prevent any possible reflection on the honour of the flag."

◼9 Churchill's Cigar

Many photographs of Winston Churchill depict him with a cigar either in his mouth or in his hand. There is even one of him at the controls of the aircraft that flew him home from Washington in January 1942, with a large cigar jutting out into the cockpit.

In November 1895, just ten days short of his 21st birthday, Churchill – who had graduated from Sandhurst at the end of the previous year and was now a second lieutenant in the 4th Hussars – accompanied his friend Reginald Barnes to Cuba, where Spanish forces were attempting to crush a rebellion by the islanders. Before leaving he persuaded the *Daily Graphic* to publish his reports on the insurrection. He also went to see Field Marshal Lord Wolseley, Commander-in-Chief of the British Army, who gave him clearance to see the Director of Military Intelligence (DMI), General Chapman. The DMI gave him maps and intelligence, and asked him to garner as much information as he could on a number of military matters, including the effect of the new metal-jacket bullet.

Few second lieutenants, then or now, would have sufficient clout to gain direct access to such elevated folk. It was an indication of the influence that Churchill had by virtue of his family connections. As well as bringing back information, he wrote to his mother, Lady Randolph Churchill, "I shall bring back a great many Havana cigars, some of which can be laid down in the cellars of 35 Great Cumberland Place" – his mother's new London home.

Churchill spent about a month in Cuba, where he filed five despatches for the *Daily Graphic*, saw some fighting and gained some sympathy for the rebel cause. On the soldierly qualities of Spanish troops, he told the *New York World*: "I make no reflections on their courage, but they are well versed in the art of retreat." During one attack, he was moving with General Valdez, who, as he later wrote to his mother, "drew

a great deal of fire on to us and I heard enough bullets whistle and hum to satisfy me for some time to come". Bullets sound, as he reported to the *Daily Graphic*, "sometimes like a sigh, sometimes like a whistle, and at others like the buzz of an offended hornet". Churchill was never to lose the taste for being near the action, of which he was to see a great deal during his life. King George VI had to write and forbid him to be present off the Normandy beaches on 6 June 1944.

The other lifelong habit he acquired in Cuba was smoking cigars: Cubans. He was as good as his word to his mother, and brought a large stock back with him. For the rest of his life he smoked between six and ten a day. He wore a cigar cutter on his watch chain, but never used it, preferring to pierce the end with a match. He was also careless with his ash, and his clothes and carpets had numerous burn marks on them.

During the Potsdam Conference (16 July–2 August 1945) after the end of the War in Europe, Stalin told Churchill that he had taken to smoking cigars. Churchill replied that if a photograph of a cigar-smoking Stalin could be flashed across the world, it would cause an immense sensation. On Churchill's return to England after the Yalta Conference (4–11 February 1945), he gave a banquet for King Ibn Saud of Saudi Arabia at Lake Fayyum in Egypt. He was told that the King, a strict Wahhabi Muslim, would not allow smoking in his presence. Churchill reported later: "I was the host and I said that if it was his religion that made him say such things, my religion prescribed as an absolute sacred ritual smoking cigars and drinking alcohol before, after and, if need be, during all meals and the intervals between them; complete surrender." The King, however, got his own back. Churchill was given a drink: "It seemed a very nasty cocktail. Found out afterwards it was an aphrodisiac," he reported.

WINSTON CHURCHILL'S CIGAR
VISIT FOR FREEDOM PICTURE
NOV. 24ᵗ 1944.

LEFT: Churchill in a "siren suit" smoking a cigar in his study.

ABOVE: A cigar half-smoked by Churchill sold at Bonhams on 17 January 2011.

◼️10 The U-boat

The terms of the 1919 Treaty of Versailles specifically forbade Germany from owning any submarines – *Unterseeboot* (hence known as U-boats). However, in 1922, the Germans set up a design bureau at The Hague in the Netherlands to ensure that they did not fall behind in submarine development. Using yards in Rotterdam and in Helsinki in Finland, they constructed submarines for export to Turkey, Spain and Finland. A number of designs were prepared which would form the basis for future German submarines. The Germans also ran a secret submarine-crew-training programme in Finnish boats. Thus, when Hitler came to power in Germany, and revoked the Versailles Treaty, it was possible to begin the construction of submarines and expand the number of U-boat crews without delay.

In January 1935, construction of U-boats began at Bremen in Germany. The first boats, Type 1 A, were based on those built for Finland and Spain. On 25 March 1935, Germany announced her intention to re-arm. Ten Type VIIA boats, based on earlier designs, were built within ten months. These were the basis of the highly successful Type VII B and VII C boats that became the workhorse of the German navy, and operated in the Battle of the Atlantic from 1939 to 1943.

Like the submarines of any navy in the Second World War, U-boats only dived when necessary. They had good endurance and surface speed when using their diesel engines. Using electric batteries when it dived, a typical submarine could motor for about one hour at around eight knots, or for four days at two knots. But the air became foul after about a day submerged, despite oxygen supplies and CO_2 absorption equipment, which the Germans were the first to develop. When the batteries became too low to provide power, the submarine had to surface to start diesels and recharge. The surface range of large submarines motoring on diesels without refuelling was many times that of any destroyer. The big German Type VII C had a range of 23,300 kilometres (12,600 nautical miles), and 59,300 kilometres (32,000 nautical miles) for the even bigger IX D. The Germans used large Type XIV *Milchkuh* or "Milch Cow" submarines as tankers to extend the range of their boats in the South Atlantic and Mediterranean.

By mid-1942, the Allied development of centimetric airborne radar, carried in very-long-range aircraft covering large areas of the Atlantic, made surfacing at night very hazardous for all U-boats, including "Milch Cows". The Germans, searching for a solution, remembered that they had found the answer on Dutch submarines captured when they overran Holland in 1940. This consisted of a pipe that could reach the surface from a dived submarine at periscope depth. A valve at the top closed the pipe automatically when the submarine dived or an unexpectedly large wave covered the top, just as the ball in a recreational diver's snorkel does today. By mid-1944 about half the U-boat fleet had been fitted with these *Schnorchels*. But there were problems with *Schnorchel*-fitted boats: the boat could not exceed about six knots or the *Schnorchel* would break off; and sometimes the valve would stick in the closed position, so the diesels sucked air from inside the boat until the engine shut down for lack of oxygen, meanwhile causing a vacuum in the boat resulting in very painful eardrums and even deafness among the crew; and finally, the noise of the running diesels blanked out the boat's sound-detection that warned of approaching enemy escorts.

The Germans constantly sought improvements to their boats in order to frustrate the Allies' increasingly effective anti-submarine measures. The Type XXI Electro boat, with greatly increased battery capacity, had a top submerged speed of 17.2 knots, and a range at five knots of 676 kilometres (365 nautical miles) without using its *Schnorchel* except to refresh air in the boat. Luckily for the Allies, this type arrived too late to take part in active operations. Even more fortunately, so did another German invention: a boat with a turbine propulsion system supplied with oxygen and steam from the chemical reaction of hydrogen peroxide. It needed no air from outside the boat, and was the forerunner of the nuclear boats of today.

LEFT: A German U-boat captain tracking his target through the periscope.

ABOVE: The U-505 in the Atlantic west of Africa after its capture on 4 June 1944 by a US Navy Task Force consisting of the escort carrier USS *Guadalcanal* and escorts.

■ The Maginot Line

At the outbreak of the Second World War, the French relied heavily on the Maginot Line, either to deter Germany from invading or to frustrate any attempts to do so. It was named after the War Minister from 1929 to 1932, who as Sergeant Maginot had been wounded at Verdun during the First World War. Loss of some of the forts defending Verdun had nearly cost the French the battle. Their experiences there and during other battles in the First World War, and the terrible losses they suffered, persuaded the French that fortresses and artillery were the answer in any future war. They fell into the age-old trap of planning to fight the next war on the basis of the previous one.

Constructed between 1930 and 1935, and extending from Luxembourg to the Swiss border, the Maginot Line was not really a line but a string of concrete forts built about five kilometres (three miles) apart and interspersed with smaller casemates. Both types were well buried, with only observation cupolas and gun turrets visible, and even these in many cases could be lowered flush with the roof. Advanced-warning posts, anti-tank obstacles, wire and mines screened the forts. The garrisons varied from about 12 to 30 men in each casemate, and from 200 to 1,200 in the forts. The latter were like underground villages, with barracks, kitchens, generators, magazines and even electric railways to transport men and ammunition from barrack and magazine to the gun positions. Casemates contained machine guns and one 47-mm (1.85-in) anti-tank gun, with heavy artillery in the forts.

Belgium was still an ally of France when the Maginot Line was being built, and so extending the line to cover the 400 kilometres (250 miles) of the Franco–Belgian border was considered tactless, as it would send a signal of no confidence in Belgium's capability to resist invasion and would isolate her on the "wrong side" of the line. An added

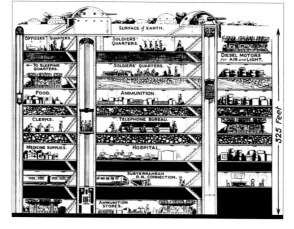

disincentive to extending the line was cost. The 139 kilometres (87 miles) completed by 1935 had cost 4,000 million francs, an overspend of 3,000 million francs. Finally, an extension of the line would run through the heavily industrialized region of Lille-Valenciennes, causing major disruption to French industry. To avoid losing this region, as they had in the First World War, the French decided that they would have to stop the invader before he crossed the French frontier. So when Belgium naively decided to opt for a policy of strict neutrality, the French planned to enter Belgian territory from the west the moment the Germans invaded from the east, with or without Belgian permission. When Belgian neutrality did not spare them from invasion in May 1940, the French were allowed in, but instead of fighting from behind the concrete and steel of the Maginot line on which so much treasure had been spent, they were forced to engage in a mobile battle of encounter in open country, a contest for which they were neither mentally prepared nor organized.

This would have been unsettling enough, but the German armoured advance through the supposedly "impassable to armoured vehicles" Ardennes, which sliced the French armies in half, was the final straw that broke the French. They had deployed their best formations into Belgium, and thus deprived themselves of the means to form a reserve. When Winston Churchill flew to Paris to find out what was happening, he asked General Maurice Gamelin, commander of all French land forces, "Où est la masse de manoeuvre?" (Where is your strategic reserve?), to which Gamelin replied, "Aucune" (There isn't one). The soldiers who might have formed a reserve were sitting uselessly on the Maginot Line. Although at the last minute some troops were pulled out of the line, they possessed neither the training nor the equipment in the shape of amour or mobile artillery to fight as a strategic reserve against a highly mobile enemy.

LEFT: A drawing of the Maginot Line that appeared in a British illustrated magazine in January 1940. It was a piece of propaganda aimed at reassuring the British public by depicitng the impregnable Maginot Line with its stocks of food, medical supplies and underground hospital. The internal railway was actually of a much more modest size.

ABOVE: In the foreground, a steel gun or observation cupola, which could be lowered flush with the ground during a heavy artillery bombardment. In the background a concrete casemate housing heavier artillery.

BELOW: French officers show visiting British officers the Maginot Line.

12 Civilian Gas Masks

oth well before and during the first two years of the Second World War, it was believed that any attack on the United Kingdom would include gas. This was because it had been used frequently during the fighting in the First World War against troops in the field, although never against civilians. Furthermore, proponents of air power, such as the Italian General Giulio Douhet, had forecast the use of gas against cities. He and others were responsible for most of the predictions that aerial bombing would cause the rapid collapse of any populations subjected to it. In the event, these predictions proved wildly exaggerated, but among those who believed them were Britain's political leaders. Their fears were fed by the RAF's insistence that the bomber would always get through, a claim that helped in the battle with the other services for funding. Along with Douhet, they proved to be wrong.

In September 1939, the only power to have an offensive gas capability

was the Soviet Union. The Germans had about 2,900 tons of gas but no means of delivering it, as Hitler had banned its use. As the war progressed, they also developed a variety of lethal nerve gases, but never used them. Despite these facts, the British believed that such weapons would be used against their civilian population, and perception was everything. British gas protection, detection and decontamination equipment were rated the best in the world. By 1938, gas masks for the civilian population were being manufactured in such quantities that by September 1939 some 38 million gas masks had been issued to households all over the country.

Everyone was required to carry their gas mask in its cardboard container with them at all times. Posters exhorting them to do so were widespread, as were instructions on how to don the mask. There were special masks for children and for babies. Wardens carried wooden gas rattles that would warn of an impending gas attack. A bell would signal the All Clear.

Civilians were not issued with protective clothing of any kind, so had mustard gas, for example, been used, their exposed skin would have been badly blistered. Thus, despite the universal issue of masks, and penalties for not carrying them, the protection measures instituted in Britain were not as effective as they might at first sight seem.

As the war progressed, people stopped carrying their gas masks, and soldiers, who in 1940 were never seen without them, stopped carrying them too. Paradoxically, this was just as the Germans were starting to develop the nerve agent Tabun, and by the end of the war an even more deadly gas, Sarin, was ready for production, with the deadliest of them all, Soman, under development. Neither the civilian population nor the armed forces of any Allied nation had clothing capable of giving protection against nerve gas.

In the event, the gas masks issued to the civilian population of Britain were never needed, and fear of retaliation prevented the Germans from using nerve gas.

ABOVE: An air raid warden gives directions to a mother and two children during a gas drill in Southend.

LEFT: A poster reminding people to carry their gas masks at all times and showing the correct way to hold it before pulling it on.

BELOW: A gas mask of the type issued to the civilian population of Britain.

Hitler will send no warning – so always carry your gas mask

ISSUED BY THE MINISTRY OF HOME

13 The Mitsubishi A6M Zero

The Mitsubishi Zero, the most famous of all Japanese aircraft of the Second World War, was the first carrier-based aircraft to outperform contemporary land-based fighters. Its appearance when Japan attacked Pearl Harbor, and during the next year of the war, came as a great shock to the Americans and British, who had failed to note its performance in China in late 1940 and ignored reports by the US General Claire Lee Chennault, commander of the Flying Tigers operating in support of Chinese forces, a year before America came into the war.

The A6M Zero was built by Mitsubishi in response to the Japanese navy's demand for a fighter with a top speed of 500 kph (311 mph) and fitted with two cannon and two machine guns. It was put into production in 1940, the Japanese year 2600, so it became popularly known as the Zero-Sen (Type 0 fighter), and to its enemies it was the "Zero", although its

official Allied codename was "Zeke". It first flew operationally in China in mid-1940 and in the first year of the war the Zero swept away Allied fighter opposition so completely that the Japanese began to believe it was invincible.

The Zero was light, manoeuvrable and had exceptionally long range. Its maximum speed at 563 kph (350 mph) exceeded the original specification and it had a range of 3.060 kilometres (1,900 miles) with a drop tank. The American equivalent carrier fighter had a range of 2,820 kilometres (1,750 miles). The Zero was able to operate from island bases if a carrier was not available; for example, during the Guadalcanal Campaign (7 August 1942–February 1943), Zeros were able to fly from islands 1,050 kilometres (650 miles) away from the combat area. At low speeds, the lightly built Zero could easily out-turn its heavier American opponents. At the beginning of the war it could climb twice as fast as its

rivals. It was one of the most agile fighters ever built and in the hands of its well-trained navy pilots it was deadly, able to match any fighter in the world. This led the Americans to adopt the saying, "Never get into a dogfight with a Zero."

It had one drawback: in order to achieve this performance, and carry heavier guns than its rival US and British fighters, it sacrificed protection. The Zero pilot was not protected by armour, nor did the aircraft have self-sealing fuel tanks. By the end of 1943, when the Zero was starting to lose its edge over American fighters, notably the Grumman F6F Hellcat, the Japanese produced the A6M5c Zero. Improvements included

a large canvas flotation bag in the rear end of the fuselage in case the aircraft ditched, mainly for use on take-off or landing in the vicinity of the carrier. It had a 20-mm (0.8-in) cannon and 13.2-mm (0.5-in) heavy machine gun on each wing, as well as a heavy machine gun over the engine, which fired through the propeller. But other than armoured glass in the cockpit, it still had no armour or self-sealing fuel tanks. The improvements made to the Zero were not enough to enable it to take on the Hellcat with any great chance of success.

As the tide turned against Japan, this great fighter aircraft was mainly used in the suicide Kamikaze role.

14 The 88-mm Gun

The German 88-mm gun, the anti-tank weapon most feared by the Allies in the Second World War, was originally produced as an anti-aircraft, or *flak* gun – *flak* being German slang for *Fliegerabwehrkanone* or anti-aircraft gun. In its anti-aircraft version, thousands of 88s were produced during the war. It had a very high muzzle velocity and ceiling (the distance up in the sky to which it could shoot). Although not as powerful as the nearest British equivalent, the 3.7-in (94-mm) heavy anti-aircraft gun, the 88's high muzzle velocity and hence flat trajectory was what made it such a formidable anti-tank gun.

The Germans first realized the potential of the 88 as an anti-tank weapon during the Spanish Civil War (1936–39) when the German Condor Legion employed it against armoured vehicles. During the 1940 Battle for France, the British and French faced this weapon for the first time, as the German army order of battle in France and Flanders included *flak* battalions. The Germans found

that their 37-mm anti-tank guns could not penetrate the frontal armour of the British Matilda MkII and French Char B tanks, whereas the 88-mm shell could. Perhaps the most dramatic demonstration of this occurred during the British counter-stroke at Arras on 21 May 1940, where the British met Erwin Rommel for the first time in the war, when he was a major-general commanding the 7th Panzer Division. Rommel personally ordered his anti-aircraft guns to fire on the British tanks attacking Wailly, southwest of Arras, bringing the British advance to a dead stop.

The British were slow to learn. The Germans repeatedly used the 88 in North Africa to devastating effect, a favourite ploy being to pull their armour back through a shield of well-concealed 88s, which then shattered the British tanks following as if they were hunting a fox. By now the anti-tank version of

the 88 had been officially designated *Panzerabwehrkanone* or PAK for short, meaning anti-armour gun.

In Russia, the 88 proved to be the only anti-tank gun able to penetrate armour of the Soviet T34; except at very close range, shells from German 37-mm and 50-mm anti-tank guns bounced off. The flat terrain of Russia suited the characteristics of the 88 perfectly, as did the desert. It was less effective in the *bocage* in Normandy or the mountains of Italy, although still greatly feared.

The versatility of the 88 was never better demonstrated than during the battle codenamed Goodwood, 18–20 July 1944, during the Normandy campaign. This operation was an attempt by three British armoured divisions to break out into open country east of Caen. The rolling country, interspersed with small woods and villages, was very different to the *bocage* further west. After making good progress, the British 11th Armoured Division was approaching the village of Cagny, when mayhem ensued.

Cagny was occupied by four 88-mm *flak* guns of the 16th Luftwaffe Field Division. Also in the village was Colonel Hans von Luck, a battle group commander of 21st Panzer Division. He ordered the Luftwaffe officer in command to engage the approaching British armour. When the Luftwaffe officer demurred, von Luck prodded him in the stomach with his pistol, saying, "You can either die now, or later winning a medal." The 88s were duly switched from pointing at the sky and re-laid on the approaching tanks. The 11th Armoured Division lost a total of 126 tanks that day, many of them to the 88s.

The 88-mm was arguably the best anti-tank gun on either side in the Second World War. It was also mounted in several types of armoured fighting vehicle, notably the Nashom, Ferdinand and Jagdpanther tank destroyers and the Tiger tank.

LEFT: An 88 on an anti-aircraft mount, a *flak* 36 cruciform, engages armour in Russia.

ABOVE: An 88 gun on wheeled mount, easy to tow and quicker to deploy than on anti-aircraft mount; especially useful in the anti-tank role.

■₁₅ The Little Ships

The role of the "little ships" in the evacuation of the British Expeditionary Force (BEF) from Dunkirk between 26 May and 4 June 1940 is perhaps the thing that most people remember about the event.

In 1940, Dunkirk was the biggest harbour on the Channel coast. It had seven deep-water basins, four dry docks and eight kilometres (five miles) of quays. When the decision was made to evacuate the BEF, the port was under almost continuous attack by the Luftwaffe and fires and extensive damage made the quays unusable. A plan was therefore put forward to take the troops off the 16 kilometres (ten miles) of beach east of Dunkirk. These shelved gently, so even small craft could get no nearer to the waterline than about a hundred metres/yards, and soldiers had to wade out to them. There were no jetties, fishing harbours or piers. Large vessels had to anchor well offshore, and craft ferrying troops to them had a long turnaround time. Clearly the more small craft, the quicker the job would be done.

The officer responsible for organizing the evacuation (Operation Dynamo) was Vice Admiral Bertram Ramsay, the Flag Officer Dover. He arranged for the Admiralty Small Boat Pool to gather at Ramsgate as many small craft as could be found: tugs, trawlers, dredgers, fishing boats (some still under sail), cockle boats, yachts and small motor cruisers whose owners loved "messing about in boats". Here their skippers, mostly their owners, were issued with charts, many of them with the course to Dunkirk already laid out for them. Many skippers had never crossed the Channel before and their knowledge of navigation was sparse; some had never even left the Thames. Navigation was made more challenging by the fact that the direct course for Dunkirk ran near Calais, which was occupied by the Germans who shelled any vessel that came within range, making an alternative "dog leg" course necessary. British minefields laid in the Channel were an additional hazard, and it was necessary to keep to the swept route.

Admiral Ramsay's representative ashore at Dunkirk was Captain W G Tennant, with a beach party of 12 officers and 150 ratings. His arrival on 27 May coincided with repeated German air raids. By the end of that day it was apparent that evacuation from the beaches was desperately slow. By midnight on 27/28 May, only 7,669 men had arrived in England, and about two-thirds of these had loaded in Dunkirk harbour before its use was suspended. But Tennant spotted that the 1,600-metre/yard-long East Mole protecting Dunkirk harbour was connected to the beaches by a narrow causeway, and that evening he ordered a destroyer to come alongside the Mole, followed by six more. The gamble succeeded, and this became the principal means of evacuation. Late on the afternoon of 28 May, the first "little ships" appeared off the beaches. The evacuation gained momentum. Nevertheless, 30 May was the only day

on which more men were lifted from the beaches (29,512) than from the harbour (24,311), and the day's total was the largest so far. The job of the "little ships" was to ferry troops out to waiting ships offshore. The courage displayed by civilian crews ploughing back and forth hour after hour, day after day, in the face of bombing was unquestionable.

At 14.23 hours on 4 June, the Admiralty gave the signal ending Operation Dynamo. Originally it was thought that some 45,000 soldiers might be rescued; in the end a total of 338,226 was reached. That the contribution of the "little ships" to the successful evacuation from the Dunkirk beaches was significant is without doubt, but their role has become the enduring myth of the operation to the extent of obliterating the contribution of the Royal and Merchant Navies. This can be understood in the context of the time – to boost national morale and cohesion, the story of the "little ships" was milked as hard as possible. The facts are that over two and a half times as many troops were taken from Dunkirk harbour than from the beaches, and of those taken off the beaches, the majority were transported in destroyers or other ships, albeit in many cases ferried out to these larger vessels, either by "little ships" or ships' boats. The actual number of men taken directly from the beaches to England by the "little ships" was small.

LEFT: Low tide on the beaches between Dunkirk and La Panne; British troops await evacuation.

ABOVE: One of the Dunkirk "little ships", moored in Rye harbour.

OVERLEAF: A river motor cruiser gets a tow from a trawler, both laden with troops from the Dunkirk beaches.

16 The Airborne Smock

Among the specialized items of equipment issued to British airborne troops in the Second World War, perhaps the most popular with the troops themselves was the airborne smock. The first pattern was modelled on the German parachutist's jump jacket, which was made to be stepped into and pulled up like a pair of overalls, except that the legs were cut off just above the knee. This was replaced by the "Smock Denison Airborne" (listed as such in the quartermaster's stores), designed by Major Denison. This was a camouflage-pattern, cotton, semi-waterproof garment that was put on and removed over the head like a jersey. It had a zipped collar, which opened as far down as the lower chest, knitted woollen cuffs and four external pockets, two on the chest and two below the waist. The inside of the collar was lined with khaki flannel.

It had a tail on the back, which could be taken up between the legs and fastened by press-studs inside the front skirt of the smock, to prevent the skirt riding up. The tail sometimes rubbed uncomfortably when the wearer was running about in the field, and soldiers left it unfastened, hanging down. Arabs in North Africa referred to the soldiers of the 1st Parachute Brigade as "the men with tails". A later version of the smock had press-studs on the back of the skirt so that the tail could be folded back and fastened to the back.

The Denison Smock was worn over the standard issue battledress. It was an excellent garment and highly prized not only by airborne soldiers but also by commandos, who were issued with it in late 1944. Its outside pockets, and the fact that it covered the wearer's nether regions, made it a considerable improvement on battledress, which had been introduced in 1939. This had been modelled on fashionable

ski outfits of the late 1930s and was not a clever design for a fighting soldier. The blouse had insufficient pockets, provided no cover for the nether regions, and after a few minutes crawling about often detached from the trousers. The map pocket on the front of the trousers, instead of the side, made extracting maps difficult while lying down taking cover. Many parachute soldiers modified their battledress trousers by sewing a capacious pocket on the side.

The Denison smock was worn under webbing equipment, small pack and ammunition pouches. However, it was found that parachute rigging lines occasionally snagged on equipment after the parachutist had left the aircraft, causing accidents and even fatalities. This led to the introduction of a sleeveless canvas over-smock, with full-length zip, and tail, which was worn over the equipment and Denison Smock. The over-smock had big elasticated pockets on the skirt for grenades, safer than descending with them clipped on the braces of the webbing – and gave the wearer a "pregnant" appearance. It was discarded after landing, and frequently the long zip was cut off and used to convert the Denison Smock to a full-length zip garment.

The Denison Smock was popular among senior officers, including those who had no connection with airborne forces but could use their influence to obtain an item of clothing that was supposed to be confined to parachute and commando troops. Montgomery frequently wore a full-zip version with a fur collar, as did General Miles Dempsey commanding the British Second Army.

The Airborne or Denison Smock was an example of a really good piece of kit, and was worn by airborne soldiers and commandos until the late 1970s.

LEFT: Soldiers of the British 6th Airborne Division fitting parachute harnesses on top of over-smocks and Denison Smocks before emplaning in Dakotas for Exercise Mush, 21–25 April 1944, a rehearsal for the Division's forthcoming task on 6 June 1944.

ABOVE: The second version of Denison Smock, with zip collar opening to the lower chest, flap and button closing at the wrists instead of knitted woollen cuffs.

⬛ 17 The Cross of Lorraine

The double-barred French Cross of Lorraine dates back to the days of the Crusades. It was worn as a heraldic device by the Knights Templar, an order of warrior monks who played a prominent part in the Crusades. At that time the two crossbars were of equal length and placed equidistant down the shaft of the cross. Later, another version came into use, on which the two crossbars were placed near the top of the shaft, the top bar being shorter than the lower bar. The Cross of Lorraine was part of the coat of arms of the province of Lorraine. Following the French defeat in the Franco–Prussian War (1870–71), the northern part of Lorraine, along with Alsace, was annexed to Germany between 1871 and 1918. To many Frenchmen, the Cross of Lorraine became a symbol of the provinces lost to France and their determination to regain them. This they achieved following the First World War, only to lose them again in 1940.

Just before the fall of France in June 1940, the hitherto little-known French colonel, Charles de Gaulle, was promoted to brigadier general and appointed under-secretary for national defence. He was the most junior general in the French army. In this capacity he met Churchill twice at conferences between British and French ministers. He made a strong impression on the British Prime Minister, which was to bear fruit when France asked Germany for an armistice on 16 June. De Gaulle was flown to England in an RAF aircraft, and authorized to broadcast an appeal on BBC radio to Frenchmen to continue the fight. A few days later, the British government recognized de Gaulle as the leader of all Free Frenchmen, "wherever they may be", and agreed to finance the Free French forces. At this juncture, a French naval officer, Capitaine de Corvette (Lieutenant Commander) Thierry d'Argenlieu, suggested to General Charles de Gaulle that the Free French adopt the Cross of Lorraine as a symbol of resistance against the Germans with their Nazi Swastika. The Cross was borne on the tricolour flags of Free French warships, on their aircraft and on their uniforms.

To begin with, the most significant response to De Gaulle's appeal to join the Free French was a death sentence from the French government, now situated in the town of Vichy, whence it administered the rump of France left unoccupied by the Germans. In mid-August 1940 the Free French Army consisted of a mere 2,240 officers and soldiers. The first gleam of hope came when the colonies of French Equatorial Africa declared for de Gaulle in early 1941, partially sparked off by a British Long Range Desert Group patrol. This gave de Gaulle a base in Africa, and from there General Philippe Leclerc marched to join hands with the British in the Western Desert.

Despite this success, the years leading up to the complete liberation of France in autumn 1944 saw relations between de Gaulle and the British, and later the Americans, follow a roller-coaster pattern: up one day and down the next. In truth, the British never really trusted de Gaulle; and he did not improve matters by being aloof and exceedingly difficult at times. He was kept in the dark about the forthcoming invasion of French North Africa in November 1942. The Allies dealt exclusively with former Vichy French senior officers; and for a time it seemed that he would be shunted off into a siding.

But clever political footwork led de Gaulle to regain command of all French armed forces in liberated parts of the world, including North Africa, by March 1944. Despite this, he was told neither the date nor the place for the invasion of Europe in June 1944. However, following a visit to Washington in July 1944, his Committee for National Liberation (CLFN) was recognized by the British and Americans as the authority in liberated France. He entered Paris on 26 August 1944 and was acclaimed by the people of Paris.

His relationship with Churchill in particular, and his British allies in general, is encapsulated in the remark made by a friend of Churchill's, Louis Spears, after de Gaulle had been especially obdurate at the Allied conference at Marrakech on 12 January 1944: "The hardest cross that Britain had to bear was the Cross of Lorraine."

LEFT: Free French propaganda poster with "France never gave up the fight" superimposed on the Cross of Lorraine and, anti-clockwise from top left, engagements and campaigns in which Free French forces took part: Bir Hacheim during the Gazala battle in the Western Desert, Fezzan in southern Libya, Tunisia, Corsica, Italy and the liberation of France. **ABOVE:** The Cross of Lorraine.

ABOVE: General Charles de Gaulle wearing a Cross of Lorraine badge above his left breast pocket.

RIGHT: The cover of a booklet issued by the French Ministry of War celebrating the liberation of Alsace and Lorraine between November 1944 and February 1945 by the French First Army under General Jean de Lattre de Tassigny.

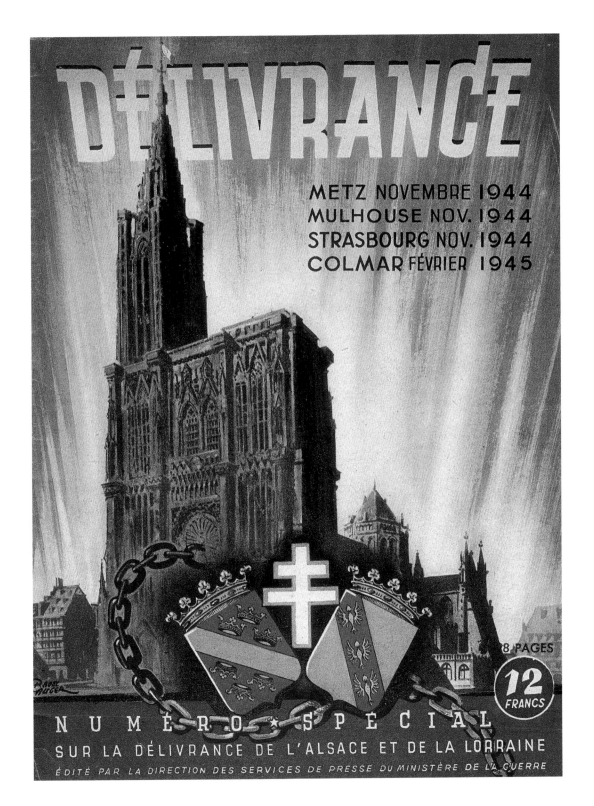

DÉLIVRANCE

METZ NOVEMBRE 1944
MULHOUSE NOV. 1944
STRASBOURG NOV. 1944
COLMAR FÉVRIER 1945

38 PAGES

12 FRANCS

NUMÉRO ★ SPÉCIAL
SUR LA DÉLIVRANCE DE L'ALSACE ET DE LA LORRAINE
ÉDITÉ PAR LA DIRECTION DES SERVICES DE PRESSE DU MINISTÈRE DE LA GUERRE

18

The Spitfire

The Supermarine Spitfire is the most famous British aircraft ever built. It was among the fastest and most manoeuvrable fighters of the Second World War and served in every theatre of that war. One of the most beautiful aircraft ever produced, it was designed by R J Mitchell, the chief designer at Supermarine Aviation Works (part of Vickers Armstrong Aviation) in response to a British Air Ministry specification to produce a fighter capable of 404 kph (251 mph). He was not satisfied with his initial designs, and it was not until March 1936 that the first successful prototype took off from Eastleigh Airport (now Southampton Airport) piloted by Joseph "Mutt" Summers, Chief Test Pilot for Vickers. In June 1936, the Air Ministry placed the first order for 310 Spitfires. Although Mitchell

died the following year as a result of cancer, he lived long enough to see his prototype fly.

Mitchell's design, the Spitfire MK1A, the first all-metal stressed-skin fighter to go into production in Britain, was an eight-gunned aircraft with elliptical wings powered by a Rolls Royce Merlin engine. Spitfires were hand-built and took three times as long to assemble as their main rival, the German Messerschmitt Bf 109E. But it was produced in sufficient numbers to play a key role in the Battle of Britain (July–October 1940). With a top speed in level flight of 570 kph (360 mph), it was comparable to the Messerschmitt BF109E (569 kph/354 mph), but more manoeuvrable in a tight turn, provided the pilot could withstand the G forces on his body. The bulged canopy gave the pilot a better all-round view than the Bf 109E, but the latter was faster

LEFT: A Supermarine Spitfire Mk VB with two 20-mm cannons and four 8-mm machine guns, all wing-mounted.

ABOVE: British fighter pilots running to their Spitfires when their squadron has been scrambled.

in a dive than the Spitfire MK1A, and had a higher ceiling, thanks to its fuel-injected engine. The Bf 109E's 20-mm cannon gave it a significant range and hitting power advantage over the Spitfire MK1A. In 1941, Spitfires came into service with two similar-sized cannon and four machine guns. The engine was constantly modified during the war, and in the later versions the Rolls Royce Griffon had twice the power of the original Merlin.

Eventually, 22,890 Spitfires of 19 different marks were built between 1936 and 1947. Although used as a fighter until the end of the war, its main role became high-level photo-reconnaissance. The United States Army Air Force flew more than 600 Spitfires during the Second World War.

The Spitfire was modified to operate off carriers, and the Seafire, as it was called, played a significant part in air battles fought by the Royal Navy's Fleet Air Arm, especially in the Mediterranean during the North African campaign in 1942–43. The last of the 2,556 Seafires produced flew in the Korean War (1950–53) with considerable success.

The last mark of Spitfire produced during the Second World War was the MkXIX reconnaissance version, with a pressurized cockpit and wing tanks to give it a 2,896-kilometre (1,800 mile) range compared with the Mk1A's range of 635 kilometres (395 miles). In April 1954 the MkXIX flew the last-ever RAF Spitfire sortie over Malaya.

◼19 The Messerschmitt Bf 109

First produced in January 1937, long before any production Hurricanes or Spitfires, and thanks to its participation in the Spanish Civil War (1936–39), the Messerschmitt Bf 109 was a thoroughly combat-proven aircraft by the time of the Munich crisis in September 1938. Earlier versions were the 109 B, C and D (the original prototype being Type A), but by the outbreak of the Second World War the 109E was available in ever increasing numbers. Nicknamed the "Emil" by its pilots, the 109E outclassed all other fighters except the Spitfire during the first couple of years of the war.

It was a small aircraft, cheap to produce and very manoeuvrable, with a fast rate of climb and dive, and high acceleration. It was normally fitted with two, or sometimes three, 20-mm cannon as well as two machine guns, which gave the 109 greater range and hitting power than fighters carrying eight machine guns, notably the earlier Marks of

Spitfires and Hurricanes. As the war progressed, the 109E and succeeding models were fitted with a variety of weapons including rockets and bombs. It had very narrow landing gear, specifically designed to allow wings to be removed for repair or replacement without having to place the fuselage on jacks; and to allow maintenance to be carried out on forward airstrips with minimal facilities. The narrow landing gear resulted in a pronounced swing on take-off and landing, which in the hands of an inexperienced pilot sometimes ended in a crash.

The cockpit was narrow with a poor forward view through armoured glass, and some pilots complained about the cramped conditions. One 109 ace, Adolf Galland, designed a higher cockpit hood named after him and fitted in the K series 109s.

The 109E, with a top speed of 569 kph (354 mph), was marginally slower than the Spitfire Mk 1A (570 kph/360

A Bf 09 at altitude, where it performed best.

LEFT: Messerschmitt Bf 109E; fighters of this Mark were known as "Emils" by their German pilots.

OVERLEAF: A Messerschmitt Bf 109E on the ground in 1941.

mph) at some altitudes, but faster in a dive and at very high altitude thanks to its two-stage engine supercharger. The Spitfire could turn more tightly than the 109E. The climb rate of the 109E was impressive: 1,005 metres (3,300 feet) per minute, compared with the Spitfire Mk 1A at 771 mpm (2,530 fpm) and Hurricane at 668 mpm (2,260 fpm). The 109-E outclassed the Hurricane (518 kph/322 mph) under all conditions.

Although it had control of the skies over Poland and France in the first year of the war, certain aspects of the Battle of Britain combined to limit the 109's effectiveness. If allowed to cross the Channel at around 9,100 metres (30,000 feet) and engage the Spitfires and Hurricanes on their own, the 109s proved superior. But the RAF turned the Hurricanes on the German bombers, dealing death and destruction at small loss to themselves. This forced the Luftwaffe to change tactics

and order the 109s to escort the bomber stream if they were not to take unacceptable losses in their bomber force. Tied to the bombers, the 109s, without drop tanks (which were introduced later), could spend only 30 minutes over England, and were unable to fly high and use their superior diving and climbing speed to advantage. Their two-stage supercharger made the 109 far more effective at high altitude than their rivals. It is possible that had the Battle of Britain been fought at 9,100 metres (30,000 feet) the RAF would have lost.

Radar also gave the British an overpowering advantage by giving ample warning of the approach of raids, which the Germans had totally discounted in their strategic calculations. To engage the RAF, the German aircrew had long flights over water and a similar return trip. All these factors limited the effectiveness of the ME 109. The happy days of almost uncontested skies over Poland and France were gone.

20 The Fairey Swordfish

The Swordfish was obsolete before it entered service. It was an open cockpit, fabric and wire-braced bi-plane, looking like a survivor from the First World War rather than an aircraft of the Second. But it served throughout the Second World War in a variety of roles, and did magnificent work. It was designed as a torpedo attacking aircraft and carried one 18-in torpedo. Its maximum speed was a mere 222 kph (138 mph), but it had a respectable range of 1,694 kilometres (1,028 miles) and could carry as good a weapon load as the Japanese carrier-borne bomber, the B5N Kate, and a far better one than the American Douglas Devastator. The latter was more advanced, but far less effective than the Swordfish, which was the most successful British torpedo bomber of the war, sinking more ships than all the Royal Navy's battleships added together.

The Swordfish usually had a crew of three: pilot, observer (navigator in RAF parlance), and a radio operator/air gunner. His single Vickers K .303-in machine gun was no match for a modern fighter. The pilot communicated with his crew through a voice pipe, known as a Gosport tube. The Swordfish was nicknamed the "Stringbag" because, like the household shopping bag of the time, it seemed to be able to carry anything and was infinitely flexible and indestructible. It could be patched up much more quickly than more sophisticated aircraft.

On 11 November 1940, 21 Swordfish were launched from the carrier *Illustrious* 285 kilometres (180 miles) from the Italian fleet main base at Taranto. They attacked in two waves, an hour apart. Surprise was complete; one new and two old battleships were torpedoed, a cruiser was hit, and the dockyard damaged. Two Swordfish were lost, but the balance of maritime power in the Mediterranean tilted in favour of the Royal Navy. The Commander-in-Chief Mediterranean Fleet, Admiral Andrew Cunningham wrote:

The 11th and 12th November 1940 will be remembered

for ever as having shown once and for all that in the Fleet Air Arm the Navy has a devastating weapon. In a total flying time of about six and a half hours carrier to carrier, twenty aircraft inflicted more damage upon the Italian Fleet than was inflicted on the German High Seas Fleet in the daylight action of Jutland. (*Engage the Enemy More Closely: The Royal Navy in the Second World War*, by Correlli Barnett, Hodder & Stoughton, 1991, page 249)

One outcome of the attack was not so welcome. The Japanese took note that battleships could be attacked in harbour by torpedo-carrying aircraft, and duly put this into effect a year later at Pearl Harbor.

Six months after Taranto, the Swordfish struck another devastating blow. The German battleship *Bismarck*, having sunk the British battle cruiser *Hood* in the Denmark Strait on 24 May 1941, was heading for Brest to repair damage inflicted in the battle. A Swordfish strike launched from the *Victorious* early on 25 May failed to damage the *Bismarck* further. As the *Bismarck* neared Brest, and Luftwaffe fighter cover, the Home Fleet battleships pursuing her in heavy seas were running short of fuel and lagging 210 kilometres (130 miles) behind. But the *Ark Royal* in Admiral James Somerville's Force H was about 65 kilometres (40 miles) north-east of the *Bismarck*. A Swordfish strike was launched and one torpedo hit the *Bismarck*'s rudder, crippling her. The Home Fleet battleships caught up and sank her.

Swordfish were also extensively employed in the anti-submarine role carrying a radar set and rockets. The aircraft could carry depth charges, mines and bombs, and its long endurance enabled it to remain on patrol over convoys for hours. A total of 2,391 Swordfishes were built between 1934 and 1944. The last front-line Swordfish squadron was disbanded on 21 May 1945, two weeks after VE Day. The "Stringbag" had outlasted many of its more modern rivals.

LEFT: Royal Navy Fleet Air Arm Swordfish in formation.

ABOVE: Despite its antiquated appearance, the Swordfish could deliver a torpedo to devastating effect, as it could bombs or depth charges.

21 An Air Raid Shelter

In 1937, government officials predicted that in any future war with Germany, bombing raids on the civilian population would cause massive casualties. The German air raids on the United Kingdom in the 1914–18 war had killed 1,413 people; next time, it was estimated, Germany would bomb the United Kingdom immediately war broke out and continue the assault for 60 days. Each ton of explosive dropped would kill or wound 50 people, a total of almost two million casualties. The fact that these statistics flew in the face of reason, not least because the Germans would be incapable of mounting an air assault of these proportions, was not material: they galvanized the government into taking a number of precautions.

In 1938, the Munich crisis led to the digging of trenches in public parks and by the outbreak of war, enough covered trenches were available to shelter half a million people. At the same time, Anderson shelters were issued. This was intended

to be erected in a town or suburban back garden and to accommodate six people. It was designed by William Paterson, and named after the Lord Privy Seal, John Anderson, who was responsible for British civil defence. The Anderson shelter consisted of 14 panels of corrugated galvanized steel: six curved panels formed the roof, six straight ones the walls and two straight panels were erected at each end, one fitted with a door. The resulting upside-down U-shaped structure was 1.8 metres (6 feet) high, 1.37 metres (4 feet 6 inches) wide, and 1.8 metres (6 feet 6 inches) long, and

internal fitting out was left to individual householders. It was buried 1.2 metres (4 feet) deep and the roof was covered with about 0.4 metres (15 inches) of soil; the earth roof and walls were often planted as gardens.

Anderson shelters were issued free to householders who earned less than £250 a year; anyone with a higher income had to pay £7. Up to the outbreak of war, some 1.5 million shelters were distributed, and a further 2 million after that. The Anderson shelter did provid good protection except against a direct hit by a bomb, but as the war progressed and all-night alerts became more frequent, it was found that, particularly in winter, many people were reluctant to go to a damp, cold hole in the ground which often flooded.

Because many houses lacked cellars, Herbert Morrison, the Minister of Home Security, decided that there was a need for an effective indoor shelter. The result was the Morrison shelter, devised by John Baker. It was issued in kit form to be bolted together inside the house, and consisted of a cage 1.8 metres (6 feet 6 inches) long, 1.2 metres (4 feet) wide, and 0.75 metres (2 feet 6 inches) high, with a steel top, wire mesh sides and a steel floor. The shelter was designed to protect people against the upper floor of a typical two-storey house falling on them if the house collapsed through blast, but it was unlikely to save their lives if the house received a direct hit. A family could sleep in the cage at night, and use it as a dining table on other occasions. Over half a million

LEFT: Damage caused by the first night raid on London on 24/25 August 1940; the house has been destroyed, along with the Anderson shelter in the garden.

ABOVE: A family uses its Morrison shelter as a dining table, as envisaged by its designer, John Baker.

RIGHT: A German photograph of two Dornier Do 217 bombers over the Silvertown area of London in 1940. Fires have started in the gasworks at Beckton. West Ham greyhound track is in the centre of the picture.

Morrison shelters were issued in the course of the war and they were highly effective, saving many lives.

Some householders built their own brick and concrete shelters in their gardens. In addition to the small shelters intended for household use, larger shelters of concrete were built in some communities to provide protection for local inhabitants who lacked alternative means of taking cover from bombing.

Before the outbreak of war, and until the night raids on London in September 1940, taking cover in Tube stations in London was banned on health grounds, the main justification for this being the spread of disease through lack of sanitary facilities. However, on the night 19/20 September thousands of Londoners took the matter into their own hands and went to the Tube stations for shelter. The government recognized defeat and took steps to make the use of Tube stations as efficient as possible, including closing off short spur sections of Underground and concreting over the tracks there, and fitting 79 stations with bunks and chemical toilets.

ABOVE: Londoners asleep on the platform at Piccadilly Tube station during an air raid.

RIGHT: A row of houses in Stepney, London gutted by bombs dropped in a night raid.

◼22 HMS *Hood*

At 46,680 tons deep load and 262 metres (860 feet) long, the battle cruiser HMS *Hood* was the largest ship ever built for the Royal Navy, and at the outbreak of the Second World War, the biggest warship in the world. Launched on 22 August 1918, she was not completed in time to take part in the First World War. Her design included modifications intended to compensate for some of the faults in battle cruiser construction exposed by the loss of three British battle cruisers in one afternoon at Jutland in 1916. Despite this, by the mid 1930s it was recognized that she still lacked armour protection in comparison with the newer capital ships being built by the Americans and Germans. But the outbreak of the Second World War in 1939 led to the cancellation of the planned reconstruction. Modifications were carried out in 1937 and 1938, but these were largely confined to anti-aircraft armament. The *Hood's* high speed, impressive size and beautiful lines concealed grave weaknesses, none of which were rectified by her final refit from January to March 1941. They included a lack of armour and a much-reduced top speed thanks to machinery defects. When she emerged from refit, she could achieve only about 46 kph (25 knots) instead of the 59 kph (32 knots) she clocked up in sea trials in 1920.

The outbreak of the Second World War found the *Hood* as flagship of the Home Fleet battle cruiser squadron. After the fall of France in June 1940, she became flagship of Force H in the Mediterranean, where she took part in the destruction of part of the French fleet in Oran on 3 July 1940. Returning to the Home Fleet in September, and after a refit in early 1941, she re-joined the Home Fleet based at Scapa Flow in the Orkneys. It was from here on 22 May 1941 that the *Hood*, flying the flag of Vice-Admiral Lancelot Holland, sortied in company with the brand-new battleship *Prince of Wales* to engage the German battleship *Bismarck*. On 18 May, Admiral Günter Lütjens in the newly commissioned *Bismarck* had sailed from Gydnia in the Baltic for the Atlantic, accompanied by the heavy cruiser *Prinz Eugen*, to attack British merchant shipping. The *Bismarck*,

armed with eight 38-cm (15-in) and 12 15-cm (5.9-in) guns, displacing 42,500 tons and with a top speed of 54 kph (29 knots), was the most formidable ship then afloat. No single ship of the Royal Navy could both catch her and destroy her. At this stage in the war the potential of carrier-launched aircraft had not been fully appreciated by the British, and Holland's squadron did not include a carrier, although a follow-up force, under C-in-C Home Fleet Admiral Sir John Tovey, did.

At 5.35 hours on 24 May, the cruiser *Norfolk*, which had been shadowing the enemy through the Denmark Strait, reported Lütjens's position at the same time as Holland, coming up to the southwest of Greenland, spotted him. Holland steered at high speed to engage the enemy. Both the *Hood* and the *Prince of Wales* were taking waves of green water over the bows as they smashed into high seas. Spray blinded their main range-finders, and the *Prince of Wales's* gunnery radar was jammed by her own high-power radio transmitting the enemy movement report to the Admiralty in London. The German and British ships opened fire at 5.53 am at a range of 23,000 metres (25,000 yards). Unfortunately, the *Hood* directed her fire at the *Prinz Eugen*, so the *Bismarck* received only half the weight of fire Holland had available. The loss of his squadron's most important advantage – its heavier broadsides – was exacerbated by the fact that neither the *Hood's* nor the *Prince of Wales's* initial salvoes were effective, whereas the *Bismarck* hit the *Hood* heavily with her second or third salvo, and at 6 am, just as Holland had ordered a turn to port to unmask the *Hood's* after turrets, *Bismarck's* fifth salvo found its mark. *Hood* blew up with a massive explosion, and only three of her crew of 1,419 officers and men survived. The precise cause of her destruction is still argued about to this day.

The *Prince of Wales* hauled off after taking seven hits, but had hit the *Bismarck* twice, damaging her fuel tanks. This was to have important repercussions because Lütjens decided that, as his flagship's endurance had been much diminished, he would abandon his Atlantic sortie and head for France.

LEFT: The last known picture of HMS *Hood*, taken from the *Prince of Wales* as both steamed into action to engage the *Bismarck*.

BELOW: The "mighty" *Hood*, as she was known in the Royal Navy, viewed from astern, showing her two twin after 38-cm (15-in) turrets. She had two forward turrets of the same design.

◼ 23 The Parachute X-Type

Britain's first parachute troops started training in the summer of 1940 in response to Winston Churchill's directive of 22 June, which asked for "a corps of at least five thousand parachute troops". To begin with, jumpers were trained using the RAF parachute designed for emergency use, operated by pulling a ripcord after leaving the aircraft. The person jumping had to estimate when to do so and have his hands free to operate it. This method was, however, soon found to be unsuitable for army parachute troops, who would be required to jump in groups from the lowest height consistent with safety while carrying heavy equipment. The parachute school at Ringway therefore changed to a parachute of American design, the statichute.

After 135 descents, one man was killed when he became entangled in the rigging lines of his parachute. The American statichute, which their airborne forces used in a modified form throughout the War, was designed so that as the parachutist jumped and fell, the static line connected to the aircraft pulled the canopy out of the bag on his back, followed by the rigging lines, the cords connecting the canopy to the harness. If the jumper made a bad exit, twisting and tumbling before the lazy cord – the final tie connecting the canopy to the static line – broke,

he risked being entangled in his own rigging lines. At best, he would then descend hanging by one or both feet and would land on his back or his head. At worst he would get wrapped up so badly that the parachute would not deploy at all. British parachute soldiers did not jump with reserve 'chutes in the Second World War, so if this happened he would die. Even if all went well, the jumper always experienced a testicle-tweaking shock as he was brought up with a jerk at the end of his rigging lines.

Raymond Quilter of the GQ Parachute Company found the remedy. Working with Irvin's Parachute Company, he produced the combination of an Irvin parachute in a GQ packing bag. This X-type parachute, which was to be the standard parachute until the 1960s, worked using a different sequence of opening. As the man jumped, the parachute pack itself broke away from his back, remaining attached to the static line and the aircraft. As the man continued to fall, his weight pulled first his lift webs – the canvas straps attaching the rigging lines to the harness – and then the rigging lines out of the bag. Finally, at the end of the taut and extended rigging lines with the jumper 6 metres (20 feet) below the bag, the canopy pulled out of the bag, the final tie which held the apex of the canopy to the pack broke, and the parachute was fully extended, leaving pack and static line attached to the aircraft. The opening shock was negligible and the danger of becoming entangled greatly reduced. The next 24,000 drops were made without a single accident.

Despite the success of the X-type, as the number of parachute soldiers requiring training increased, a team from the Airborne Forces Experimental Establishment and the Royal Aircraft Establishment monitored the procedures followed at the Parachute Training School. As a result, it was decided that twisting and somersaulting in the slipstream could be reduced if a new design of pack was introduced, in which the strap which connected the parachutist to the static line in the aircraft pulled out of the pack at the level of his neck, rather than at waist level. Some accidents still occurred because canopies made of silk sometimes failed to open properly when the material adhered to itself through static electricity. This problem was solved by changing to canopies made of nylon.

The X-type parachute was the standard type used by British airborne forces throughout the Second World War. Of a total of more than half a million descents made in training at No 1 Parachute Training School with this statichute up to August 1948, only 42 fatal accidents occurred: a ratio of one in 12,000.

LEFT: A parachutist at the moment of landing. His feet are not together, risking a broken ankle and a reprimand.

ABOVE: Back view of a parachutist in a steel helmet, wearing an X-type parachute. The "D" ring at the end of the strap is to connect it to the static line in the aircraft.

■24 The Sten Gun

During the 1940 campaign leading up to the fall of France, the British Expeditionary Force (BEF) encountered an enemy armed with sub-machine guns, principally the German MP28. A British soldier armed with a bolt-action rifle, especially at close quarters, was at a disadvantage against a German equipped with a sub-machine gun with automatic fire; officers and specialists such as despatch riders armed only with a revolver, even more so.

Following the evacuation of the BEF, there was a pressing need to manufacture small arms to make up losses incurred in the campaign, as well as to equip a rapidly enlarging army. The British bought as many Thompson sub-machine guns (Tommy guns) from the United States as could be spared from America's own programme to re-equip their expanding armed forces, but this made up only part of the shortfall. The Royal Small Arms Factory at Enfield was therefore charged with producing a British sub-machine gun. The design selected was the Sten, an acronym formed from the first letter of the surnames of the designers (Major Reginald V Shepherd and Mr Harold J Turpin) and the first two letters of Enfield.

The Sten was cheap and easy to manufacture and could be turned out in small workshops by relatively unskilled labour. Eventually there were eight marks, including models with suppressers or silencers. The Mark III, which was the cheapest and simplest, consisted of only 47 parts and took five man-hours to assemble.

The magazine was side-mounted, copying the German MP28, but this made the gun awkward to hold and fire, especially from the waist, as the firer had to either curve his left wrist under the magazine to grip the fore end or hold the magazine. The latter was discouraged as the vibration caused by automatic firing against the lever effect of the hand holding the magazine could distort the poorly manufactured magazine catch, altering the angle of the magazine and so causing the round to misfeed and jam. It was not unknown for the magazine to be wrenched out of its socket, leaving the firer holding the gun in one hand and the magazine in the other – embarrassing if not fatal. Despite this being well understood, there are numerous photographs of troops taken in the Second World War holding their Stens by the magazine.

The Sten worked on the blow-back principle: the explosion that sent the bullet up the barrel also blew back the bolt, so only half the energy of the explosion was used to send the round on its way. This, combined with the type of 9-mm $(1/3$-inch) ammunition used, meant that the Sten had poor penetrating power. Earlier marks had no safety catch and as a consequence the Sten was sometimes more dangerous to its owner and to friends standing around than to the enemy – wounds and fatalities from accidental discharges were commonplace. Even if the weapon was not cocked, banging it hard on the butt or dropping it butt-down could cause the bolt to drive back sufficiently far for it to pick up a round from the magazine when the spring reasserted itself and pushed the bolt forward. Once the round was seated in the breech, the fixed firing pin on the bolt fired the round, blowing back the bolt to repeat the process until the magazine was empty. To prevent this from happening, later marks had a hole drilled in the casing to take the cocking handle.

Despite these imperfections, millions of Stens were produced during the Second World War, and on the whole it was a successful weapon in the right circumstances. It was suitable for close-quarter battle, but ineffective at ranges above about 90 metres (100 yards), and therefore useless in open country.

LEFT: A posed photograph of British Paratroops at Oosterbeek, Holland, September 1944, in the battle for Arnhem. Shown here holding their Sten guns by the magazine.

ABOVE: A Mark III Sten with skeleton butt.

■25 The T-34 Tank

The T-34 was the most significant Soviet tank of the Second World War. Its inventor, Mikhail Koshkin, named it the T-34 because he first conceived the basics of its design in 1934. Some 40,000 were built during the Second World War, and it was the most advanced design of its time anywhere in the world. Prototypes were completed in early 1940, and production started immediately, stimulated by the German invasion of France and the Low Countries, even though the Soviet Union was not at war at the time. The T-34 was fast and had fully sloped armour which was thicker than that of any contemporary German, British or American tanks, with a low silhouette. Its main armament as the vehicle developed was the formidable 76.2-mm L40 gun. Its wide tracks and Christie suspension (with wheels connected to springs) gave it a low ground pressure and hence good terrain-crossing ability, even in mud and snow. This was critical in Russia, and in this respect it was far superior to any German tank. Its V12 diesel engine was also less flammable than the petrol engines in German tanks.

Simple to maintain and operate, the T-34 looks more modern than any other tank of its day. Right up to the end of the Second World War, the Germans and the British, and to some extent the Americans, were building tanks with flat front glacis plates and front turret plates. A flat surface at 90 degrees to the trajectory of an incoming round is more easily penetrated by armour-piercing shot, which ricochets off fully sloped armour like that of the T-34.

As with any armoured vehicle, you only achieve a combination of thick armour, a big gun and high speed with a trade-off. In the case of the T-34, it was size and crew space – the tank was very cramped. Until the improved T-34-85 came into service in early 1944, there was room for only two men in the turret: the commander and the loader. Most tanks in other armies had a three-man turret crew: commander, gunner and loader. A T-34 commander had to aim and fire the gun while attempting to command his tank, and in the case of platoon commanders, command his sub-unit at the same time. The commander's problems were not made any easier by the fact that few Soviet tanks were fitted with radios. Only company commanders and upwards had radios, while the rest had flags. Therefore a company commander could speak only to fellow company commanders and his battalion commander; even he had to give orders to his company using flags.

The Germans remained ignorant about the T-34 in the first few months after they invaded Russia, as few T-34s were deployed when Operation Barbarossa was launched in June 1941. To begin with, the Germans had a field day destroying several thousand Soviet tanks, but in September 1941 they met the T-34 in large numbers, and it soon demonstrated that it could outshoot, outrun and outlast any German tank. The effect was to make all German tanks obsolete. The Panzer divisions that had hitherto swept all before them in Poland, France, the Low Countries and North Africa were no longer kings of the battlefield. Field Marshal Ewald von Kleist called the T-34 "the finest tank in the world". Major General Friedrich von Mellenthin wrote later, "We had nothing comparable." But the Germans continued to inflict defeats on the Red Army until late 1942, and occasionally beyond, because until that time Soviet tactics were faulty; their command and control and operational techniques were nothing like as good as the Germans' – lack of radios being a factor – and they deployed their armour badly. An additional contributor to German continued success for a while was the introduction of new tanks, notably the Tiger heavy gun tank and the medium Panther. The T-34 remained the backbone of Soviet tank divisions to the end of the Second World War.

LEFT: T-34s taking up firing positions on the Third Byelorussian Front in 1944. Their wide tracks enabled them to operate in mud.

ABOVE TOP: The T-34. Its sloped armour gave protection against armour-piercing ammunition.

ABOVE: T-34s entering Berlin in May 1945.

OVERLEAF: T-34s moving at speed, carrying infantry. The nearest tank has a radio aerial, and is probably a company commander's tank or even battalion commander's.

26 The Atlantic Charter

ven before the United States became an official belligerent in the Second World War, President Franklin D Roosevelt worried about the common war aims of the US, Great Britain and the Soviet Union. By covenant and inference Roosevelt, Churchill and Stalin had agreed to the defeat of Nazi Germany as a common war aim. For their nations to survive and prosper, Germany would be forced to disarm, reform and submit to an international treaty regime that would forever restrict its power for imperialistic expansion and political coercion through the threat of war.

In the face of domestic opposition to entering the war or forming an alliance with Great Britain and the Soviet Union, Roosevelt, a wiser and older Wilsonian (ie committed to the idea of collective international security), wanted a general statement of war aims that would appeal to idealistic, internationalist Americans, the sort of people who wrote and read magazine and newspaper articles on foreign policy. Since Churchill and Stalin had reputations as imperialists, Roosevelt knew they had few admirers in the United States beyond Anglophiles and dedicated Communists but. FDR could at least improve Churchill's image as a firm ally and internationalist.

Between 9 and 12 August 1941, Roosevelt and Churchill met aboard warships in Placentia Bay, Newfoundland to discuss their current strategic relationship and their future plans if and when the United States became a belligerent. They also wanted to reassure Stalin they would aid him in his defence of the Soviet Union, largely by threatening Japan and saving Stalin from a two-front war. Part of FDR's bargain in aiding Great Britain with surplus US Navy destroyers and Lend-Lease supplies was to convince Churchill to sign the Atlantic Charter.

The document was a promissory pact between the United States and Great Britain that was supposed to reassure their own people and potential allies that they did not seek imperial gains in territory or economic advantage, that they believed in national self-determination and freedom of the seas.

The document also contained a hope for the future that embodied FDR's "Four Freedoms". They were: freedom from fear, freedom from want, freedom to worship and freedom of speech, announced by FDR in a speech in January 1941. Churchill, who at that point in the war would, by his own admission, have made a pact with the devil, agreed that these goals were admirable statements of principle. He did not comment on their likelihood of realization. Sharing Churchill's desperation, Stalin agreed to accept the Atlantic Charter later in the year.

Neither FDR nor Churchill actually signed an Atlantic Charter document; instead they made it a press release. However idealistic and expedient, the provisions of the Atlantic Charter eventually took on life in the Charter of the United Nations.

ABOVE: American president Franklin Delano Roosevelt with British prime minister Winston Churchill on board HMS *Prine of Wales* in Placentia Bay, Newfoundland in August 1941.

RIGHT: The final draft of the Atlantic Charter with Winston Churchill's corrections marked.

OVERLEAF: The declaration of the United Nations, signed by 26 nations, agreeing to the principles of the Atlantic Charter.

COPY NO: 1

M O S T   S E C R E T

NOTE: This document should not be left lying about and, if it
is unnecessary to retain, should be returned to the
Private Office.

P R O P O S E D   D E C L A R A T I O N

B. ALTERNATIVE VERSION - i.e. VERSION "A"
INCORPORATING NEW PARAGRAPH PROPOSED BY
CABINET IN ABBEY TELEGRAM NUMBER:- 31.

The President of the United States of America and the
Prime Minister, Mr. Churchill, representing His Majesty's
Government in the United Kingdom, being met together, deem it
right to make known certain common principles in the national
policies of their respective countries on which they base their
hopes for a better future for the world.

First, their countries seek no aggrandisement,
territorial or other;

Second, they desire to see no territorial changes
that do not accord with the freely expressed wishes of the
peoples concerned.

Third, they respect the right of all peoples to choose
the form of government under which they will live; and they
wish to see self-government restored to those from whom it
has been forcibly removed.

Fourth, they will endeavour, with due respect to their
existing obligations, to further the enjoyment by all peoples
of access, on equal terms, to the trade and to the raw
materials of the world which are needed for their economic
prosperity.

Fifth, they support fullest collaboration between
Nations in economic field with object of securing for all
peoples freedom from want, improved labour standards, economic
advancement and social security.

Sixth, they hope to see established a peace, after the
final destruction of the Nazi tyranny, which will afford to
all nations the means of dwelling in security within their own
boundaries, and which will afford assurance to all peoples
that they may live out their lives in freedom from fear.

Seventh, they desire such a peace to establish for all nations
safety on the high seas and oceans.

Eighth, they believe that all of the nations of the
world must be guided in spirit to the abandonment of the use
of force. Because no future peace can be maintained if land,
sea or air armaments continue to be employed by nations which
threaten, or may threaten, aggression outside of their
frontiers, they believe that the disarmament of such nations
is essential pending the establishment of a wider and more
permanent system of general security. They will further the
adoption of all other practicable measures which will lighten
for peace-loving peoples the crushing burden of armaments.

Private Office.
August 12, 1941

DECLARATION BY

<u>DECLARATION BY UNITED NATIONS:</u>

<u>A JOINT DECLARATION BY THE UNITED STATES OF AMERICA,</u>
<u>THE UNITED KINGDOM OF GREAT BRITAIN AND NORTHERN</u>
<u>IRELAND, THE UNION OF SOVIET SOCIALIST REPUBLICS,</u>
<u>CHINA, AUSTRALIA, BELGIUM, CANADA, COSTA RICA, CUBA,</u>
<u>CZECHOSLOVAKIA, DOMINICAN REPUBLIC, EL SALVADOR,</u>
<u>GREECE, GUATEMALA, HAITI, HONDURAS, INDIA, LUXEMBOURG,</u>
<u>NETHERLANDS, NEW ZEALAND, NICARAGUA, NORWAY, PANAMA,</u>
<u>POLAND, SOUTH AFRICA, YUGOSLAVIA.</u>

The Governments signatory hereto,

Having subscribed to a common program of purposes
and principles embodied in the Joint Declaration of
the President of the United States of America and the
Prime Minister of the United Kingdom of Great Britain
and Northern Ireland dated August 14, 1941, known as
the Atlantic Charter.

Being convinced that complete victory over their
enemies is essential to defend life, liberty, independence
and religious freedom, and to preserve human rights and
justice in their own lands as well as in other lands,
and that they are now engaged in a common struggle
against savage and brutal forces seeking to subjugate
the world, DECLARE:

(1) Each Government pledges itself to employ its
full resources, military or economic, against those
members of the Tripartite Pact and its adherents with
which such government is at war.

(2) Each Government pledges
with the Governments signatory h
a separate armistice or peace wi

The foregoing declaration ma
other nations which are, or whic
material assistance and contribu
for victory over Hitlerism.

*Done at Washington
January First, 1942*

*The Unit...
by t...
The United K...
a Northern
by Wins...
on behalf
of the Union ...
Republics
Max...

National Gover...
T...

The Commonwe...
by Rich...

The Kingdom...
by ...
Canada ...
by Lei...*

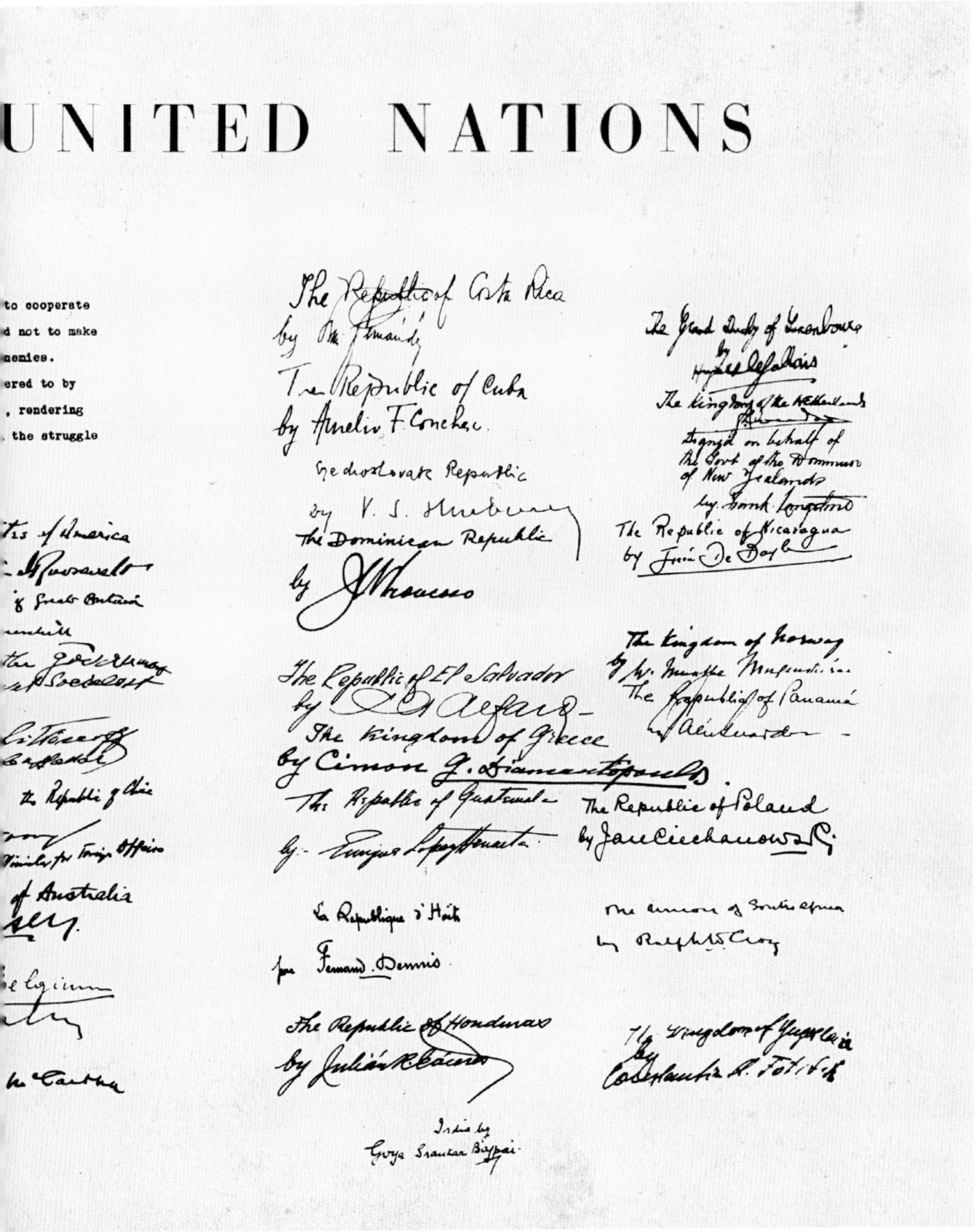

UNITED NATIONS

to cooperate
d not to make
nemies.
ered to by
, rendering
, the struggle

tts of America
— M Roosevelt
g Great Britain
urchill
the Government
of Soodeloot

Littooff
of Barkall
the Republic of Chile

inister for Foreign Offices
of Australia
lely.

Belgium

u Cartha

The Republic of Costa Rica
by Oca Fernande,

The Republic of Cuba
by Amelio F. Conchar.

Czechoslovak Republic
by V. S. Hurbery

The Dominican Republic
by J Henessro

The Republic of El Salvador
by E A Alfaro

The Kingdom of Greece
by Cimon G. Diamantopoulos

The Republic of Guatemala
by Enrique Lopytumate

La République d'Haïti
par Fernand Dennis.

The Republic of Honduras
by Julián R Cáceres

India by
Girja Srancan Bajpai.

The Grand Duchy of Luxembourg
by Hugues Lefaivre

The Kingdom of the Netherlands
Bloon
Signed on behalf of
the Govt of the Dominion
of New Zealand
by Frank Langstone

The Republic of Nicaragua
by Juan De Bayle

The Kingdom of Norway
by W. Munthe Morgenstierne

The Republic of Panamá
by Alawarder

The Republic of Poland
by Jan Ciechanowski

The Union of South Africa
by Ralph W Close

The Kingdom of Yugoslavia
by Constantin A. Fotitch

73

■ An Air Raid Warden's Helmet

27

In Second World War Britain, a man or woman wearing a helmet with a big W painted on it was instantly recognizable as an Air Raid Warden. Air Raid Precautions, or ARP for short, were a series of measures set up in 1935 by the British government in response to the prediction of massive casualties that would be caused by German bombing in the event of war. The Air Raid Wardens' Service was created in 1937 and, while by mid-1938 it had grown to 200,000 strong, the Munich crisis saw another 500,000 join the Service. Most of these part-time volunteers, sometimes called ARP Wardens, had other jobs which they carried out when not engaged on Warden duties. ARP Wardens wore overalls with an armband, and a black steel helmet with a W in white lettering. Chief Wardens wore white helmets with a black W. Later in the war, all ARP Wardens wore blue serge battledress.

Contrary to government and public expectation, there were no large air raids on the United Kingdom during the first 11 months of the Second World War. One of the reasons for this was the fact that the Luftwaffe was incapable of providing fighter escorts for its bomber force all the way from Germany to the United Kingdom and back; this became possible only after airfields in France became available in June 1940. Without air raids, there was little for Air Raid Wardens to do in those early months other than enforce the blackout regulations, which led to the image of the Warden as a self-important busybody of the kind portrayed by Chief Air Raid Warden Hodges in the popular UK TV series *Dad's Army*. However, they came into their own during the Blitz in 1940–41; along with other Civil Defence, Casualty Service and Fire Service men and women, the Air Raid Wardens performed devotedly, and often with heroism.

The Civil Defence Service included rescue and stretcher parties, control centre staff and messenger boys; the Casualty Service comprised emergency ambulance workers and first-aid-post staff. The Fire Service was made up of full-time and part-time regular firemen, and part-time auxiliaries. Full- and part-time police officers, and hundreds of thousands of members of the Women's Voluntary Service (WVS), were also part of Civil Defence.

In London, Air Raid Wardens were based at local posts placed at about ten to a square mile. They patrolled regularly, reporting the locations of bombs as they fell. If it was an incendiary bomb, they would attempt to smother it with sandbags. They supervised the public shelters and were in effect the "eyes and ears" of Civil Defence. Rescue teams summoned to bomb-damaged areas included stretcher-bearers and "heavy rescue men"; the majority of the latter were building workers familiar with house construction.

While patrolling the streets, Air Raid Wardens ensured that no light was visible from any of the buildings in their "patch". On seeing a light, they would call out, "Put out that light," and regular offenders were reported to the police. They helped to police bomb-damaged locations, and gave immediate assistance to bomb victims. They were trained in firefighting and first aid, and attempted to keep a situation under control until the rescue services arrived.

Two ARP Wardens were awarded the George Cross for gallantry during the Second World War. The first-ever recipient of the newly created George Cross was ARP Warden Thomas Alderson on 30 September 1940; ARP Warden Leonard Miles was awarded his posthumously, on 17 January 1941.

LEFT: A Chief Warden (left) and a Warden help an injured woman to a reception centre from a first-aid post after her home in Liverpool was bombed on 6 May 1941.

ABOVE: A warden's helmet.

28 The Mosin-Nagant Rifle

The Mosin-Nagant rifle was in service for over 100 years, first with the Imperial Russian Army, then the Red Army, and finally the Northern Alliance forces in Afghanistan in 2001. Experience in the Russo–Turkish war of 1877–78, where the Turks were using Winchester repeaters and the Russians single-shot rifles, persuaded the Imperial Army that modernization of their small arms was overdue. Captain Sergei Ivanovich Mosin submitted a design for a 7.62-mm ($1/3$-in) magazine-fed rifle, in competition with a rifle designed by a Belgian, Léon Nagant. After some deliberation, the commission formed to decide which rifle should be adopted by the Imperial Army chose Mosin's design, but as the final production model of 1891 incorporated some features of Nagant's design, the rifle was designated the Mosin-Nagant M1891. Production was started both in Russia and in France. By the outbreak of the Russo–Japanese War in 1904, about 3.8 million Mosin-Nagants had been delivered to the Imperial Army, but few were actually used, as scarcely any soldiers had been trained to use them.

Because of the poor state of Russian industry at the outbreak of the First World War, a shortage of Mosin-Nagants forced the government to place orders for M1891s with two companies in the USA: Remington and Westinghouse. The first consignment arrived just as the 1917 October Revolution broke out, followed by the Russians signing the Treaty of Brest-Litovsk with Germany and its allies, which took Russia out of the war for a while. To avoid the risk that the next consignment would fall into the hands of the Germans or

Austrians, the US Army bought the remaining quarter of a million Mosin-Nagants. These rifles were used to equip the British and US forces sent to northern Russia in the anti-Bolshevik campaign of 1918–19.

The Mosin-Nagant was used by both sides in the Russian Civil War of 1918–24, and by the Finns in the "Winter War" of 1939–40 against the Red Army. The Mosin-Nagant was the standard-issue weapon for the Red Army when Hitler invaded Russia in 1941. By the end of the Second World War about 17.4 million M1891s had been produced. The Mosin-Nagant was highly popular, and easy to maintain; Russian soldiers called it just the Mosin, or "Mosinka". It was also modified as a sniper rifle and used by the famous Red Army snipers, notably at Stalingrad (1942–43) but in all other battles too. The Finns also used the sniper model against the Red Army: one Finnish sniper claimed over 500 kills with a Mosin-Nagant.

After the Second World War, the Soviet Union ceased producing Mosin-Nagants, progressively replacing them with the AK series of assault rifles. However, the M1891 was used in many of the campaigns that followed the Second World War: Korea (1950–53), Vietnam (1955–75) and Afghanistan (2001–present). Every country or insurgent group that received military aid from the Soviet Union used some Mosin-Nagants, including Egypt, Syria, Iraq and Palestinian terrorist groups.

Through its long service life, eight models of Mosin-Nagant were produced. In addition several countries, including Finland, Czechoslovakia, China, Hungary, Romania and Poland, manufactured variants.

ABOVE LEFT: The Mosin-Nagant rifle

ABOVE: Red Army infantry with Mosin-Nagant rifles jump down from
a T-34 in December 1942.

29 The SAS Cap Insignia

In October 1941, Lieutenant David Stirling of the Scots Guards, attached to Number 8 Commando, part of Colonel Robert Laycock's Force Z, was lying in a Cairo hospital, temporarily paralysed from the waist down following a parachuting accident. The army commandos of Force Z were bored and frustrated. Raids had been cancelled, or had gone awry. Participation in the final stages of the battle for Crete, where they had not exactly covered themselves in glory, was the final straw. Force Z was disbanded at the end of July 1941.

Stirling pondered how best to improve the raiding operations in which Number 8 Commando had been engaged with so little success. He concluded that the numerous enemy bases, particularly airfields, strung out over hundreds of miles behind their lines were ideal targets. The way to get at them was by the two open flanks: the desert to the south, the sea to the north. The latter had been used as an approach by commandos, but their raids had been wasteful in resources, even scarcer now since the losses suffered by the Royal Navy in the Greece and Crete evacuations in 1941. Poor planning by amateurs in the amphibious art had led to failures. Perhaps a number of smaller parties, each of no more than four or five men inserted by parachute, submarine, fishing boat or vehicle, would have a greater chance of achieving surprise, and could attack a number of targets simultaneously.

He committed his idea to paper. When fit to walk, he bluffed his way in to GHQ Cairo, and was eventually summoned by General Claude Auchinleck, C-in-C Middle East, who promoted him to captain and told him to raise a force of 65 men who would be dropped behind enemy lines. The force was to be known as L Detachment Special Air Service Brigade, a totally imaginary formation that existed only in the fertile brain of Brigadier Dudley Clarke who was responsible for deception in the Middle East. He was trying to persuade the Germans

that a fully equipped airborne brigade was stationed in Egypt. Real parachutists, albeit a mere 65 men and the only ones at that in the whole Middle East, were the icing on the bogus cake Clarke was baking.

The first raid, on 16–17 November 1941, was a disaster. High winds and sandstorms resulted in all the SAS men being dropped miles from the dropping zones (DZs). Eventually 22 men including Stirling, out of the 55 who had dropped, turned up at the rendezvous manned by Captain David Lloyd Owen of the Long Range Desert Group (LRDG). He argued that Stirling should in future let the LRDG take them to the target; eventually Stirling agreed. For the next year, until the SAS got their own jeeps, the LRDG, the desert experts, provided a "taxi" service.

The SAS now began to achieve some notable successes, mainly raiding airfields. Time after time they destroyed every aircraft on the airfields they hit. Captain "Paddy" Mayne's personal score was higher than any Allied air ace. When the desert campaign finished, they went on to operate in Italy, the Aegean and France. Although they sometimes parachuted into their operational areas, they used Jeeps to greater effect. Perhaps their most notable achievements were the long Jeep patrols behind enemy lines in France after the Allied invasion in June 1944.

The SAS winged dagger badge is worn to this day by the three Special Air Service Regiments (21, 22, 23), as are the distinctive straight-top SAS parachute wings. These were designed by two SAS officers: Lieutenant Jock Lewes, Welsh Guards, President of the Oxford University Boat Club, and Lieutenant Tom Langton, Irish Guards, a Cambridge rowing blue. They were modelled on the wings of the sacred ibis depicted in the décor of Shepheard's Hotel in Cairo. The light and dark blue feathers of the wings are based on the Cambridge and Oxford rowing colours, chosen by Langton and Lewes.

LEFT: An AS patrol wearing Arab headdress in the Western Desert. By 1943, the SAS was equipped with Jeeps, here mounting Vickers K guns.

ABOVE: The winged dagger SAS capbadge.

30 The Boeing B-17

At the heart of Allied strategy for the defeat of Nazi Germany, the Combined Bomber Offensive, code-named Pointblank, required the Royal Air Force and US Army Air Forces (USAAF) to destroy Germany's industrial heartland. The aircraft for this mission could not be developed overnight, and it was decisions made in the 1930s by the Ministry of Air and the US War Department that dictated the bomber types the RAF and USAAF used to strike Germany.

After underfunded, incremental bomber development following the First World War, in 1934 the US Army Air Corps asked Boeing Aircraft to develop a multi-engine bomber that could carry one ton of bombs a minimum of 1,600 kilometres (1,000 miles) and return to base. It gave Boeing no advance payment but the company would be paid if its bomber became the USAAC's choice. Boeing's Model 229 or XB-17 flew for the first time in July 1935, but crashed four months later. The

accident, which happened at take-off, killed much of the design and testing team, but the USAAC ordered 13 more aircraft because this bomber had become its highest priority.

The development of the B-17 focused on over-water flight and the bombing of an enemy invasion fleet. While such a mission seemed far-fetched for the protection of the Atlantic Coast, it was relevant to the defence of the Commonwealth of the Philippines, the Territory of Hawaii and the Panama Canal Zone. Although USAAC planners in 1939 foresaw the need for bombers to reach Germany and Japan in the future, the coastal defence mission was the only one that convinced Congress to fund the XB-17 project.

As more models received testing between 1936 and 1941, the basic character of the wartime B-17 (E and F models) took shape. The four-engine bomber (four Pratt & Whitney 1,200hp supercharged radial piston engines)

ABOVE: A B-17 bomber circa 1941.

OVERLEAF: The "Flying Fortress" being built in a Boeing factory during the Second World War.

could drive a 29,000 kg (65,000 lb) aircraft almost 3,200 kilometres (2,000 miles) at speeds up to 462 kph (287 mph) and at altitudes up to 10,700 metres (35,000 feet). The aircraft would be a "Flying Fortress" with a crew of ten, eight of whom could man an assortment of 13 turret-mounted or swinging machine guns. The bomb load for missions might run as high as 7,700 kg (17,000 lbs). The bombsight, the Norden type developed by Sperry-Rand, allowed the bombardier to fly the plane for greater accuracy, and made automatic corrections for altitude, wind and drifting.

Although the USAAC (US Army Air Forces after June 1941) ordered B-17s for operational deployment, the number of B-17s (models B-E) numbered fewer than 600 by December 1941, and did little to slow the Japanese campaign of 1941–42. Some of these models had been sent to RAF Coastal Command to attack U-boat bases. The models E and F (almost 4,000 aircraft) went to British bases in 1942 to begin the daylight bombing of Germany, but German air defences brought long distance raids to a halt in December 1943. Actual combat experience brought changes to the models G and H, principally improvements to the engine and armouring, and the addition of a chin turret to meet head-on fighter attacks. By war's end, Boeing and two other contractors had built 12,677 B-17s. Enemy air defences destroyed about 5,000 of them across all theatres of war, and hundreds more crashed in operational accidents.

31 Oboe

During the Second World War the Germans, British and Americans introduced electronic navigation systems to assist their bombers in finding the correct target at night or in bad weather. Early in the war, both sides discovered that bombing a well-defended country by day in good weather without heavy fighter escort was extremely costly. The RAF was the first to learn that its doctrine that "the bomber will always get through", so assiduously proclaimed before the Second World War, was spurious. The losses sustained by the RAF in the first months of the war persuaded the Air Staff that the only way a strategic bombing campaign against Germany could be sustained was by bombing at night. The Americans in their turn discovered that daylight bombing without using fighter protection when over heavily-defended occupied Europe was unsustainable. Their solution was to provide plenty of long-range fighter escorts.

The main problem when night bombing was locating the target. The Germans, turning to night bombing of Britain after their defeat in the Battle of Britain, were the first to light on a solution. They used a system of radio beams, initially Knickebein, but superseded by X-Gerät (X-Apparatus), and Y-Gerät. Despite these the German results were mediocre, not least because the system could be jammed. Meanwhile, the RAF's performance, without any navigational aids, was abysmal. Only one in three RAF crews placed their bombs within eight kilometres (five miles) of the aiming point; some were tens of miles off target.

In early 1942, the RAF introduced a radio system called Gee. It was not so accurate as Knickebein, but it did improve bombing accuracy until the Germans started jamming it. The

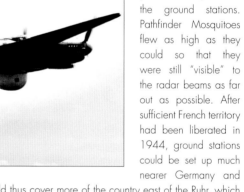

RAF's answer, in early 1943, was Oboe, so called because its radar pulses sounded like the woodwind instrument. The system used two ground stations in England. One tracked the aircraft as it flew along an arc of constant range running through the target, and passed correction signals if it deviated from the arc. The second station measured the range along the arc, and when the aircraft reached the previously computed bomb release point, a signal was broadcast. Mosquito pathfinder aircraft were fitted to receive the signals, and they marked the target with flares for the main force to bomb.

Oboe was very accurate and difficult to jam. Its one drawback was that the curvature of the earth reduced its range to about 450 kilometres (280 miles) from the ground stations. Pathfinder Mosquitoes flew as high as they could so that they were still "visible" to the radar beams as far out as possible. After sufficient French territory had been liberated in 1944, ground stations could be set up much nearer Germany and could thus cover more of the country east of the Ruhr, which had been only just within the range of Oboe stations based in England.

The installation in mid-1943 of H2S radar sets in RAF bombers, which gave a "picture" of the ground on a screen, enabled sorties to be carried out beyond the range of Oboe, although bombing accuracy depended on the quality of the radar echo. Coastal targets showed up clearly; targets inland, especially in broken terrain, were more difficult to find.

The Americans installed electronic navigation systems similar to Oboe in their bombers, to enable them to find and attack daylight targets through cloud and haze.

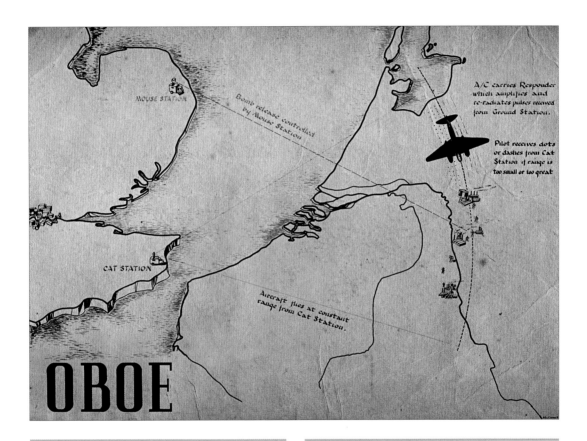

MOUSE STATION

Bomb release controlled
by Mouse Station

A/C carries Responder
which amplifies and
re-radiates pulses received
from Ground Station.

Pilot receives dots
or dashes from Cat
Station if range is
too small or too great

CAT STATION

Aircraft flies at constant
range from Cat Station.

OBOE

LEFT: A Mosquito B MkXVI fitted with a ventral raydome testing an H2S radar. This aircraft was also used to test Oboe.

ABOVE: A diagram showing the principle on which Oboe worked, with two ground stations in England tracking the Mosquito marker aircraft as it flies along the arc.

32 The Human Torpedo

The Italians were the first to use human torpedoes in the Second World War, and were swiftly copied by the British, Germans and Japanese. The Italian Maiale ("pig") was 6.7 metres (22 feet) long, with a detachable explosive nose. It had a two-man crew who sat astride the torpedo wearing rubber suits and oxygen cylinders and masks.

On 19 December 1941, two Italian frogmen were caught sitting on the bow buoy of the British battleship *Valiant* in Alexandria harbour. Under interrogation they said that they had got into difficulties outside the harbour and had had to abandon their equipment and swim. A few minutes later there was an explosion under the stern of the tanker *Sagonia*. The Italians told the captain of the *Valiant* to bring everyone on deck, as there would shortly be an explosion under his ship. He did so, and minutes later a massive explosion caused extensive damage to the *Valiant*. Soon after, another explosion severely damaged the battleship *Queen Elizabeth*. Three pairs of Italians on human torpedoes, brought to Alexandria by submarine, had immobilized the only two battleships in the Mediterranean Fleet and put them out of action for many months, though there were no casualties. The Italians also used human torpedoes to attack Allied shipping in Gibraltar, Malta and Algiers Bay later in the war.

Copying the Italian example, the British developed the Chariot, based on a 7.6 metre (25 foot) torpedo, specifically to attack the German battleship *Tirpitz* at Trondheim in Norway. On the night of 30/31 October 1942, two Chariots were taken into the Trondheimfjord slung under a fishing boat, but on the approach while still about 15 kilometres (ten miles) from the *Tirpitz*, the Chariots broke loose and sank. The Chariot crews however made their way to Sweden as planned.

On 28 October 1944, a successful attack was made by a pair of Chariots on two ships at Phuket in Siam (Thailand). The crew were taken to the target area by the submarine *Trenchant*, motored in on their Chariots, and clamped the explosive heads to the bilges of the two target merchant ships, the *Sumatra* and the *Volpi*. Having returned to the *Trenchant*, two explosions were heard, and both ships were out of action for the rest of the war. It was the last and only completely successful Chariot operation, out of a total of eight, in the whole war.

The German one-man Neger, sometimes called the Mohr after its inventor Richard Mohr, consisted of two torpedoes clamped together on top of each other. The upper one had a small plexiglass-covered cockpit instead of a warhead. It was slow and could not dive, motoring with the cockpit above the water. It had to be released close to the target, and was easily seen in daylight, often with sunlight flashing off the cockpit. Negers were used against Allied shipping at Anzio in January 1944 and again in Normandy in June. They damaged two minesweepers and a light cruiser off the Normandy beaches, but large numbers of Negers were lost. The successor to the Neger, the Marder ("pine marten") was no more successful.

The Japanese Kaiten was a converted Long Lance torpedo, which included a compartment for the crewman and a conning tower. The Long Lance was a huge torpedo, 9 metres (30 feet) long, with half a ton of explosive in the warhead, and capable of 91 kmp (49 knots). It was usually driven straight at the target as a suicide weapon. They were first used at Ulithi atoll, the US fleet anchorage, in November 1944, sinking a tanker for the loss of eight Kaiten pilots. At Iwo Jima, Okinawa and at other beachheads in the Pacific, they sank four US vessels (the largest being the destroyer USS *Underhill*). The Japanese loss rate was huge. Of the 18 submarines converted to carry Kaitens, eight were sunk either before or after launching the human torpedoes; others were forced to abort their missions. About 80 Kaitens were also lost.

The Italian human torpedo attacks were the most successful in terms of "return on investment" – the result balanced against the cost in the lives of extremely brave men, the time, expense, and effort in developing the weapon, and taking it to the target. The return on investment by the British, Germans and Japanese on human torpedoes was negligible; but this is not in any way to denigrate the courage of the men who rode the torpedoes.

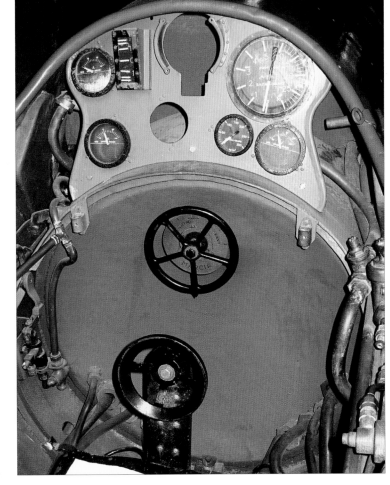

ABOVE: The Italian human torpedo, known as the Maiale (pig).

RIGHT: The controls of the "pig".

OVERLEAF: A damaged Italian human torpedo captured with the mother ship *Otterra*, a converted merchant ship was used to mount attacks against Allied shipping in Gibraltar in 1942 and 1943. After the ship was surrendered to the British in 1943, the torpedo was found in a secret compartment.

■33 Japanese Headgear

The two most familiar forms of headgear worn by the Japanese armed forces were the pot-shaped steel helmet, and the cloth field cap with its short, cloth, occasionally leather, peak. A star for the Imperial Japanese Army (IJA) and an anchor for the Imperial Japanese Navy (IJN) was welded onto the front of the helmet, and sewn on to the front of the cap.

The comfortable and practical field cap was worn with more formal uniforms, as shown in the photograph of Japanese officers attending the surrender ceremony aboard the USS *Missouri*, and as worn by General Tomoyuki Yamashita at his trial by the War Crimes Commission in Manila in October 1945. The cap was the same pattern for all ranks.

The steel helmet was often covered in a net into which foliage and grass camouflage could be inserted. Even in the equivalent of service dress, Japanese officers of all ranks often wore a tunic open at the neck, over a white shirt without a tie.

The ubiquitous field cap was symptomatic of the practical approach to kit and equipment on the part of the Japanese, especially in the IJA. For example, their soldiers were equipped with a very efficient grenade launcher which

threw a 0.8 kg (1 lb 12 oz) shell out to around 640 metres (700) yards, accurately and effectively – far better than anything possessed by the Allies.

The Japanese were trained to fight with their 38-cm (15-in) bayonet fixed to a 6.5 mm (.256 inch) calibre rifle at all times to instil fear into their enemy. Their infantry especially was recruited from the rural population, whose tough farmers made excellent soldiers. It would be wrong to imagine them as uneducated peasants, for the standard of schooling in Japan was high. They were indoctrinated to believe that they were the toughest race in the world, and that death was to be expected, not feared.

In addition to the field cap in blue cloth, Japanese seamen wore a round white hat, like those issued in the British Navy, when in white uniform, and a blue one with their blue, winter uniform. Both types of round hat had what the Royal Navy called a cap "tally" round the brow part of the cap with the name of the wearer's ship in Japanese characters. Officers and petty officers of the IJN wore blue or white peaked caps, according to the time of year. These caps were similar to those worn in most navies. Japanese sailors in working dress wore either the field cap or, when working with aircraft on carrier flight decks, a cotton flying helmet.

ABOVE: A Japanese soldier in Bataan in the Philippines after it fell.

RIGHT: An example of the typical Japanese cloth field cap.

■34 The Secret Radio

Inserting spies, agents and saboteurs into enemy territory was usually only the first phase of a clandestine operation. If they could not communicate they were probably useless. Among other things, they needed to receive instructions from base and likewise pass information back; ask for airdrops of equipment; request extraction, either for themselves or others; and vector and talk to the dropping or pick-up aircraft. The only efficient and speedy way to achieve this was by radio, or wireless as the British called it, so special radio sets had to be devised for use by agents which had to meet several important criteria.

First, the set had to be rugged and able to stand up to rough treatment. It also needed to be as small as possible in order to be easily portable, and if possible fit into a suitcase or some other innocuous container for concealment. It had to be capable of transmitting and receiving over long ranges. Ideally it needed to be able to work on batteries, mains power or a hand or pedal generator.

Some of these requirements conflicted. The technology of the time usually demanded a big radio set with plenty of power to transmit over long ranges. The transistor had not been invented at that time and all radios worked using valves, which were easily broken. Meanwhile, long-range communications normally required big antennae, which was out of the question for clandestine operations.

These problems were addressed mainly by the Special Operations Executive (SOE) in Britain, and the Office for Strategic Services (OSS) in the US, and by early 1942 sets that fulfilled the key criteria were being produced. The smallest radio for agents was the Paraset Clandestine Radio designed for SOE and the Secret Intelligence Service (MI6), weighing about 2.3 kg (5 lbs). But more reliable, and seen in many a film, was the SOE Type A, Mk III suitcase radio weighing about 6 kg (13 lbs), which had a range of 800 kilometres (500 miles). The US equivalent was the AN/PRC-1 suitcase design, weighing about 13.5 kg (30 lbs).

The radios in existence at the time were insecure; they could not automatically "scramble" their messages to prevent anyone listening in from deciphering the text. Today clandestine radios use burst transmission to send a long text message over the air in micro-seconds, giving an enemy direction-finding station too little time to fix the transmitting radio's location. The sets in the 1940s could not do this.

The high-frequency radios used by agents were unable to send and receive voice messages over long distances, so Morse code was the communicating method. Messages were enciphered using one-time pads: the sender and receiver had identical pads of tear-off sheets containing the information for enciphering and deciphering a signal, the sender transmitting the sheet number. Once the message had been sent and deciphered at the other end, both operators destroyed their copy. No other copies existed. This method was unbreakable but slow, and tapping out a long message exposed the sender to the danger of being picked up by hostile direction-finding equipment, of which the Germans had numerous high-quality sets. Many operators were caught this way.

The agent communicated with supply aircraft over an S-phone using voice transmission – radio telephone in the jargon of the day. The aircraft carried the master set while the agent carried the "ground set" which weighed around 7 kg (15 lbs), fitted in a suitcase or pack on the agent's back. The theoretical range when used as a radio telephone to an aircraft at 3,000 metres (10,000 feet) was about 65 kilometres (40 miles), down to 10 kilometres (6 miles) at 150 metres (500 feet). Ground detectors more than a mile away could not pick up transmissions to an aircraft. The signal from the set could also be used to aid in vectoring the aircraft to the dropping zone from about 130 kilometres (80 miles) away.

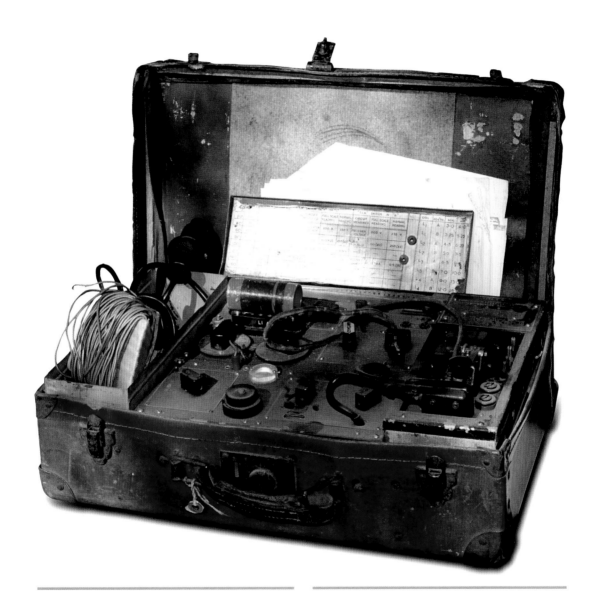

LEFT: Members of the French Resistance operating a radio.

ABOVE: The radio set used in training by Yvonne Baseden an F Section SOE radio operator. Aged 22, she was parachuted into France to join the SCHOLAR circuit operating near Dijon. Following participation in the largest daylight drop of supplies to the Resistance up to that time, she was captured on 26 June 1944, interrogated by the Gestapo, sent to Ravensbruck Concentration Camp, and liberated in April 1945. She was awarded the MBE (Military), Legion d'Honneur and the Croix de Guerre with Palm.

■ A Silk Escape Map

Silk escape maps were produced by MI9, the secret British escape service, and by MIS-X, its US equivalent. A branch of the military intelligence directorate in the War Office formed in December 1939, MI9 had several tasks: to garner intelligence about the enemy from repatriated prisoners of war (POWs) and through coded correspondence with those still in POW camps; to assist prisoners to escape, through advice given beforehand and by smuggling escape kit to them; to train the armed forces in methods of escape and evasion; and to organize groups of helpers abroad to assist escapees on their way home.

MI9 provided aircrew going on operational flights or commandos embarking on raids with wallets containing about £10-worth of local currency, a small hacksaw and a small compass. They also carried maps printed on silk, which was hardwearing and easy to conceal. A company well known for producing playing cards and board games including Monopoly, Waddington Limited, printed British escape maps. These were copied from those produced by the map publisher Bartholomew, who waived all copyright and royalties for the duration of the war.

A silk map could be concealed in a cigarette packet or the heel of a shoe, and could survive hard treatment, even immersion in water. The maps were small scale and covered a large area, and some were double sided. The range of British maps was extensive: for example, the 1943 series for the European theatre of operations consisted of ten maps, which in various combinations gave coverage of France, Belgium, Holland, Germany, Czechoslovakia, Poland, Hungary, Romania, Serbia, Bulgaria, Spain, Switzerland, Greece, Albania, Turkey, Crete and Portugal. Other series covered Norway, Italy, Cyrenaica, the Asia-Pacific theatre, in short almost everywhere in the world where British service people and agents might find themselves.

Issuing silk maps to aircrew or commandos before embarking on a mission was one thing; smuggling them to POWs was another. No maps or other escape gear were included in Red Cross food parcels in case these were banned – most POWs relied on them for survival as the rations, especially towards the end of the war, were meagre. Nor could parcels from families be used as a means

of smuggling in such kit, for it was known that they were always thoroughly searched. Fictitious charity associations were therefore set up to send parcels of games and clothing to POWs and some of these included board games, which the Germans permitted on the grounds that POWs might be less troublesome if they had something to do. There were clues as to which map was concealed so that the right maps went to the right POWs: in a Monopoly board, for example, this would be a full stop after the name of a place on the board: Mayfair, Marylebone and so forth.

The POWs had escape organizations which as well as making civilian clothes, false papers and other items of escape kit, printed maps using the silk maps as masters. These "re-prints" were drawn by hand, and reproduced using jelly from Red Cross parcels, ink from pitch and rollers from window bars. We shall never know how many maps were successfully smuggled into POW camps, but we do know that more than 33,000 British, Commonwealth and US servicemen reached Allied lines from enemy territory, either as escapers or evaders (those who had never been captured in the first place).

RIGHT: The silk escape map carried by Squadron Leader Hugh Beresford Verity RAFVR while serving in Number 161 Squadron RAF in support of the SOE.

FRANCE

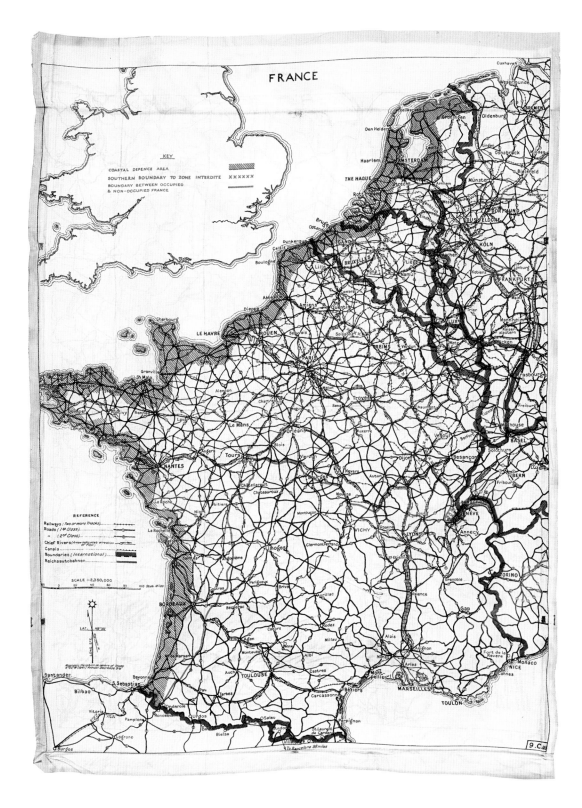

KEY

COASTAL DEFENCE AREA

SOUTHERN BOUNDARY TO ZONE INTERDITE ✕✕✕✕✕

BOUNDARY BETWEEN OCCUPIED
& NON-OCCUPIED FRANCE

REFERENCE

Railways (Two or more Tracks)........
Roads (1st Class)........
"   (2nd Class)........
Chief Rivers (Arrow indicates direction of Flow)........
Canals........
Boundaries (International)........
Reichsautobahnen........

SCALE 1:2,350,000

36 The Bombe and Colossus

The Bombe, spelt with an "e", was precursor to the first ever computer, Colossus. It was an electro-mechanical machine invented to break coded messages transmitted by the Germans. These messages were usually enciphered on an Enigma machine before being transmitted. Invented in 1923, the Enigma was used by the German Army and Navy, the Luftwaffe, the SS, the Military Intelligence Service (Abwehr) and the German State Railways (Reichsbahn). Originally it consisted of three rotors and a keyboard linked by an electric circuit, arranged in such a way that pressing a lettered key would light up a different letter on a display on the machine. Having been given the text of a message in clear, the operator would rewrite it substituting the original letters for those displayed by Enigma. The rotor settings were changed daily. Even in its simplest form, for every letter there were hundreds of millions of possible solutions. As the war progressed, an additional rotor was added, hugely increasing the number of steps that anyone deciphering the message had to get right before the message made sense. Throughout the war the Germans believed that Enigma was unbreakable.

Although a number of Enigma machines fell into British hands during the war, knowing how it worked was only the beginning; and anyway the British already possessed a similar machine known as Typex. The trick was to know the daily rotor settings. The British, recognizing that Enigma could be "broken", installed a group of university mathematicians at the Government Code and Cypher School at Bletchley Park, north of London. To begin with, the deciphering of messages was partly achieved by the application of mathematical formulae based on the fact that a) there are only 26 letters in the alphabet, b) no letter could stand for itself, and c) without number keys, figures had to be spelt out. To assist in this process, a type of machine devised by Polish code breakers, and greatly improved by a brilliant mathematician, Alan Turing, was installed at Bletchley. Nicknamed the Bombe, these machines were continually upgraded throughout the war, and eventually there were five types in use, not all at Bletchley. However it was there that the first Enigma codes were broken mechanically by the Bombe on 1 August 1940.

The Colossus, the world's first ever true computer which was devised to break the Lorenz enciphering machine code, was installed at Bletchley in December 1943. The Lorenz had 12 rotors instead of the improved Enigma's four. Eventually five Colossus machines were installed at Bletchley, some of which were used to decipher Japanese codes. The breaking of these codes provided an unexpected bonus in the form of intelligence for Allied planning for the landings in Normandy in June 1944. Early in 1944, the Japanese Military Attaché in Berlin was given a comprehensive tour of the part of the Atlantic Wall defending among other places, the beaches selected for the Allied assault. On return to his embassy, he sent a series of long messages back to Army HQ in Tokyo giving a highly detailed description of what he had seen in the minutest detail. His messages were intercepted by one of the British listening stations in England, and deciphered. The information they contained proved invaluable when read in conjunction with air photographic reconnaissance in establishing the number and calibre of guns, down to machine gun nests, defending the beaches.

ABOVE LEFT: One of the priority teams at work at Bletchley Park, handling the high priority coded radio traffic, such as signals that affected key operations including the Normandy landings.

LEFT: A Bombe code breaking machine of the type that broke the Enigma codes mechanically for the first time on 1 August 1940.

TOP: A rare picture of the Colossus with its Wren operators. The Mark I was powered by 1,500 valves, the Mark II by 2,500.

ABOVE RIGHT: A Bombe unit room at Eastcote in Middlesex. This was similar to the Bombe room at Bletchley. As the workload on the Bombe machines increased during the war, units were established at more than eight other locations in addition to Bletchley Park. By 1944, there were at least 200 machines in operation at their various sites.

37 The *Stars and Stripes*

Published as a newspaper for the soldiers of the American Expeditionary Forces in 1917–19, *Stars and Stripes* came to life again in 1942 in order to provide news of the Home Front and the global war effort to deployed GIs. The newspaper had the War Department's endorsement and financial support, but editorial control swung back and forth between on the one hand, the Army's commanders and senior public affairs officers, and on the other, the newspaper's editorial staff, most of whom were established journalists who wore uniforms but remained more loyal to the First Amendment than to the Articles of War.

Reporting news from the Home Front presented no special "freedom of speech" problems since *Stars and Stripes* relied on US news services and national newspapers for domestic news. Sound coverage of government policies and domestic events, even unpleasant ones, offset rumours, the biased views of families and enemy propaganda. *Stars and Stripes* could also give GIs a sense of the conduct of the war in other theatres, the contributions of the other services and the Allies, and the reasoning behind the Army's strategic and operational decisions as seen from the War Department. There were few revelations about operations that violated security. *Stars and Stripes* reporters followed the censorship rules on security which applied to all newsmen.

Where *Stars and Stripes* ran into trouble was among senior commanders who saw the newspaper as a subversive influence that undermined their authority and encouraged indiscipline. The *Stars and Stripes* editorial staff, however, did not regard senior officers as infallible, or all Army policies

as wise. Popular cartoonist Sergeant Bill Mauldin created his characters Willy and Joe, the iconic GIs of the Second World War, as a vehicle to criticize what he saw as the Army's tactical sophistry, and to expose the unjustified privileges for officers and rear area personnel. *Stars and Stripes* sought examples of commanders violating Army policies that advantaged enlisted men. This investigative reporting ferreted out examples of black-marketeering and misallocation of scarce supplies meant for combat units.

General Mark W Clark continually hectored military reporters. General Douglas MacArthur, as senior military commander in the Pacific, banned *Stars and Stripes* in the area until 1945. However, *Stars and Stripes* reporters could attack command influence by leaking stories to their civilian war correspondent colleagues. General George S Patton wanted Mauldin court-martialled; instead he received a Pulitzer Prize in 1945.

Stars and Stripes reached more than a million readers during the Second World War, and its reporting on the war with Germany remains an invaluable source of information about the war as fought by American enlisted men.

ABOVE: US soldiers reading an issue of *Stars and Stripes*.

RIGHT: The special edition of *Stars and Stripes* published to mark VE Day on 9 May 1945.

NICE-MARSEILLE EDITION

V-E Day **THE STARS AND STRIPES** **D+336**

Daily Newspaper of U.S. Armed Forces   in the European Theater of Operations

Vol. 1—No. 57   Wednesday, May 9, 1945   ONE FRANC

Allies Proclaim:

IT'S OVER

Surrender Is Signed At Rheims

By CHARLES F. KILEY
Stars and Stripes Staff Writer

RHEIMS, May 8 — The Third Reich surrendered unconditionally to the Allies here at Gen. Dwight D. Eisenhower's forward headquarters at 2:41 AM Monday.

The surrender terms, calling for cessations of hostilities on all fronts at one minute past midnight (Double British Summer Time) Wednesday, May 9, were signed on behalf of the German government by Col. Gen. Gustaf Jodl, Wehrmacht chief and Chief of Staff to Fuehrer Karl Doenitz.

Under Jodl's signature were those of Lt. Gen. Walter Bedell Smith, Chief of Staff to the Supreme Allied Commander; Gen. Ivan Susloparoff, head of the Russian mission to France who was authorized by Moscow to sign on behalf of Soviet forces, and Gen. Suvez of France

The surrender was signed in five minutes in the SHAEF war room here, 55 miles east of Compiegne forest where Germany surrendered in the last war on Nov. 11, 1918, and the scene of the capitulation of France to the Third Reich in this war June 21, 1940.

Flew from Germany

The terms were signed in less than ten hours after the arrival of Jodl by plane from Germany, and 34 hours after final negotiations first begun with the arrival Saturday of Gen. Adm. Hans Georg von Friedeburg, commander in chief of German navy, who on Thursday headed the Nazi delegation which surrendered German forces in Denmark, Holland and Northwestern Germany to the 21st Army Gp.

Gen. Eisenhower did not take

(Continued on Page 8)

Announce the Victory

GEN. EISENHOWER   **PRESIDENT TRUMAN**
"The crusade . . . has reached its glorious conclusion."

3rd Told Big News After Taking Prague

On the day of official announcement of the European war's end Third U.S. Army troops drove into Prague, and Marshal Joseph Stalin announced the fall of Breslau, Germany's ninth city, after an 80-day siege.

The Czech radio announced yesterday that the Czechoslovak commander of Prague defenses had welcomed the commander of the First Div. to Prague. The Germans, who fought a four-day patriot uprising, surrendered effective the afternoon of May 9—today.

A Soviet correspondent reported that the German commander raised the surrender flag at Breslau at 1800 hours Monday. German defense efforts ended in almost complete destruction of the city.

SWEDES BREAK WITH GERMANY

Sweden yesterday severed diplomatic relations with Germany on the ground that there is no central government to be recognized. The Swedish radio said all German buildings in Sweden had been taken over

Doughs Watch 'Final' Battle

ON THE ELBE RIVER, May 8— One of the last battles of the European war was fought on the east bank of the Elbe today—between the Russians and the Germans with Americans as spectators.

Everybody knew the end of hostilities was only a few hours away.

For the last week the German 12th Army was pushed back on the Elbe, and began surrendering to U.S. troops. The Germans built bridges while Americans on the west bank of the Elbe watched and accepted their surrender.

Peace came to Europe at one minute past midnight this morning (Nice-Marseille time) when the cease-fire order to which Germany had agreed went into effect.

Formal announcement of Germany's unconditional surrender came nine hours earlier in radio proclamations by President Truman and Prime Minister Churchill.

As they spoke the last "all-clear" sirens sounded in London and Paris, and the streets in both cities were the scenes of frenzied celebrations. America took the announcement calmly and quietly, having staged its celebration Monday when the German announcement of the surrender was flashed.

All hostilities had not ceased yet, however. Some German pockets still were resisting the Russians in Czechoslovakia and on islands in the Baltic Sea. Moreover, up to a late hour last night Moscow had not proclaimed victory.

The surrender agreement, it was disclosed, was signed at 0241 hours Monday in Gen. Eisenhower's headquarters at Rheims, France. To the last the Germans attempted to split the Western Allies and Soviet Russia, offering surrender at first only to the Western Allies. This was rejected flatly by Gen. Eisenhower.

Defeat of Germany—concluded in the bomb-burned and

(Continued on Page 8)

Allied Soldiers Praised In Ike's Victory Order

The text of Gen. Eisenhower's victory order of the day follows:—

Men and women of the Allied Expeditionary Force:

The crusade on which we embarked in the early summer of 1944 has reached its glorious conclusion. It is my especial privilege, in the name of all nations represented in this theater of war, to commend each of you for valiant performance of duty. Though these words are feeble they come from the bottom of a heart overflowing with pride in your loyal service and admiration for you as warriors.

". . . Astonished the World . . ."

Our accomplishments at sea, in the air, on the ground and in the field of supply have astonished the world. Even before the final week of the conflict you had put 5,000,000 of the enemy permanently out of the war. You have taken in stride military tasks so difficult as to be classed as impossible. You have confused and destroyed your savagely fighting foe.

On the road to victory you have endured every discomfort and privation and have surmounted every obstacle ingenuity and desperation could throw in your path. You firmly joined up with the great Red Army coming from the east, and other Allied forces coming from the south.

Full victory in Europe has been

(Continued on Page 8)

38 The Auster Light Aircraft

The Auster light aircraft was arguably the best airborne artillery spotter in the Second World War. It was designed by Taylorcraft in the USA for the expanding light private aircraft market, and in 1938 Taylorcraft Aeroplanes (England) was formed to build the aircraft under licence. Several variants were produced and on the outbreak of the Second World War these were evaluated for use as airborne spotters for artillery. The Taylorcraft Plus C two seater was selected for military production and designated the Auster Mk I.

The design was so successful that it was developed into the Mk III version. It was fitted with a Gipsy Major I engine, and 470 of this type were built. The next progression was to the Mk IV, with an American Lycoming engine and a larger cabin to accommodate a third seat. The fully glazed cockpit of the Mk IV and subsequent models were a great improvement on the earlier variants, which did not afford good visibility to the side and rear. But the most common Auster found with British forces was the Mk V, which included blind-flying instruments. Around 800 of these were built.

The Auster could operate off short, rough strips, and could land on roads and tracks provided obstructions on either side were removed. It had a high mounted wing, which gave excellent lift, and provided an unobstructed view of the ground. Thanks to its large trailing edge wing flaps, the Auster could fly at very low speed without stalling, which was invaluable when observation over the ground was needed. This, combined with its large rudder giving it exceptional turning ability especially at low speed, made it surprisingly difficult for a fighter to shoot down. By twisting and turning in flight and suddenly applying full flap, a skilled Auster pilot could bring his aircraft almost to a stop momentarily, and a pursuing fighter would often overshoot. The Lysander developed by the RAF for air spotting was shot out of the sky when used in this role.

The Auster Mk V with a top speed of 209 kph (130 mph) was faster than the German equivalent, the Fieseler Fi 156C Storch whose top speed was 174 kph (108 mph), and the American O-49 Vigilant (196 kph [122 mph]). The Auster also had a greater range (204 kilometres [250 miles]) than the Storch (286 kilometres [240 miles]), although it was less than the Vigilant (450 kilometres [280 miles]). Thanks to its low take-off weight (837 kg [1,846 lbs]) the Auster could operate from smaller strips, forest clearings and the like, than either the Storch (1,322 kg [2,915 lbs]) or the Vigilant (1.539 kg [3,392 lbs]). This enabled the Auster to be deployed much closer to the front line and hence its reaction time to calls for support was usually quick.

The Auster was used for reconnaissance, often by senior commanders who wanted to see the terrain over which they were going to deploy their troops, in the way that a helicopter is used today. But by far the most common use of the aircraft was to put an artillery observer up in the air from where he could correct the fall of shot. Artillery officers were taught to fly and, together with RAF pilots, were formed into joint air observation post squadrons (Air OP for short). They were able to detect and engage targets out of sight of friendly artillery observers on the ground. As an added bonus it was found that the presence of an artillery spotter aircraft often caused the opposing side's artillery to cease firing for fear of being spotted and having counter-battery fire brought down on it.

The Air OP did not fly directly over the target, but usually remained on his own side of the battlefield, while remaining high enough to see dead ground out of sight of OPs on the ground.

To begin with, the formation of the Air OP was resisted by the RAF, who were paranoid, as they are to this day, about any suggestion that the Army was forming a private air force and about any threat to the notion that only the RAF should fly every type of aircraft.

RIGHT: An Auster Mk III with a 130-hp Gipsy engine, the most widely produced of the early Auster variants.

39 The MG 42 German Machine Gun

By the end of the First World War, machine guns consisted of two types: light and heavy. The latter, such as the Vickers, Maxim and Browning, were almost all water-cooled. Although the .50-calibre Browning was invented towards the end of the war, it did not come into service with the US army until 1922. The heavy machine gun, in some armies designated "medium", was designed to be used for long-range suppressive fire in support of attacks, and to be fired at all ranges in defence from fixed positions. It fired from a heavy tripod, or in some armies, an even heavier sled, and sometimes had a shield. The condenser can for the water-cooling system was cumbersome, and if all the water evaporated and no more was available, someone might have to urinate on the gun to cool it down. The ammunition was carried in a bulky box known in the British army as a "liner", containing one 250-round belt. The whole system – condenser can, ammunition liner, tripod and gun – could not be carried by one man. Because of its bulk, such a machine gun was difficult to conceal; to have a good chance of surviving, it had to be sited in a pit dug for it, or in a fold in the ground.

Before the First World War, the American Colonel Isaac Lewis designed a light machine gun, initially manufactured by the British Birmingham Small Arms Company. It saw much service with the British and US armies in the First World War, and was still used extensively in the Second. The Lewis, able to be carried by one man (although others carried extra ammunition for it) could be fired from a prone position, or, at a pinch, while standing; it was also easily concealed. The inter-war years saw the introduction of improved light machine guns into armies: the US Browning Automatic Rifle (BAR); the British Bren (actually a Czech design); and the French-designed Vickers-Berthier

– all magazine-fed weapons. Light machine guns were all air-cooled, so that when the barrel became too hot from prolonged firing, it could be replaced with a cool spare barrel.

Most armies fought throughout the Second World War with at least two types of machine-gun: light, medium, and in some cases heavy as well. The German Army however believed that having two varieties of machine gun for different tactical roles often resulted in the correct weapon not being available. They therefore designed the first general purpose machine gun or GPMG. The basic weapon was the same, a belt-fed gun with an easily changed barrel, capable of being mounted on a tripod, and provided with long-range sights, but also with a bipod and shoulder butt. For long-range tasks the butt could be removed, the bipod unclipped, the gun quickly mounted on a tripod, and sights fitted that allowed indirect fire and night shooting on fixed lines. The advantage was that only one type of gun had to be manufactured.

The first of the type was the MG 34, designed in the early 1930s and adopted for service in 1934. It weighed 12.1 kg (26 lbs 11 oz), fired 7.92mm ammunition, and was belt- or magazine-fed, with a cyclic rate of 650 rounds per minute. It remained the German army's GPMG until 1942, when it was replaced by the more reliable and cheaper MG-42. This gun at 11.6 kg (25 lb 8 oz) weighed marginally less than the MG 34 and was belt-fed only, but had a cyclic rate of 1,200 rounds per minute, twice that of the 34. Incorrectly called the Spandau, because the original pre-First World War Maxim had been modified for use by the Imperial German Army at the Spandau arsenal, it was actually made by Mauser. The MG 42 was a greatly respected and feared weapon; its rate of fire was so fast, it sounded like a buzz saw. By contrast British and US medium and light machine guns had cyclic rates of between 450 and 550 rounds per minute. A British infantry platoon commander remembered: "When it came to a firefight between a German platoon and a British platoon, their MG 42 won hands down. I remember my first reaction to actual infantry warfare in July 1944 was one of amazement at the crushing fire-power of this very rapid-firing gun." (*18 Platoon* by Sydney Jary, published by Sydney Jary Ltd, 1987.)

Now most armies have a GPMG in their inventory.

ABOVE: An MG 42 German machine gun.

LEFT: German paratroopers fire MG 42s across the River Arno in Florence in mid-1944 during the Italian campaign.

40 PLUTO

The acronym PLUTO stands for Pipeline Under The Ocean. As early as 1942, the problem was being considered of how to supply the huge quantities of fuel required by Allied forces invading and operating in Europe. Eventually there would be around two million soldiers and airmen ashore, with thousands of tanks, trucks and aircraft all requiring fuel. Following successful trials of a pipeline laid across the floor of the Bristol Channel, the development of a system to be laid in the English Channel went ahead. The final design was a 75-mm (3-in) diameter steel pipe welded into continuous lengths each of 48 kilometres (30 miles), and rolled onto big floating drums – Conundrums – from which the pipe would be laid. The Conundrums looked like giant cotton reels, 27.5 metres (90 feet) long and 15 metres (50 feet) in diameter, and when carrying a full length of pipe, weighed as much as a destroyer.

Starting at the Isle of Wight, the Conundrums were towed across the Channel, laying four lengths of pipe to Cherbourg after its capture by the Americans. Pipes were also laid from Liverpool to the Isle of Wight, over land except for the section in the Solent. These allowed fuel to be landed at Liverpool and pumped to Cherbourg.

PLUTO was unable to provide fuel for the Battle of Normandy in 1944 and the breakout operations, a period of over three months, because the first four pipelines, codename Bambi, could not be deployed until enemy minefields around the port and in the Cotentin Peninsula had been cleared. Pumping operations began on 18 September, by which time the Allied armies were hundreds of miles away on a line stretching from Holland and Belgium to the borders of Germany, and the Vosges.

Meanwhile fuel for the fighting was provided by Operation Tombola. This involved petrol being pumped ashore from small tankers off the Normandy coast along buoyed pipelines, direct to storage tanks at the British pipehead at Port-en-Bessin and the American one at Ste Honorine. These pipelines had a daily capacity of 8,000 tons. Fuel packed in jerry cans was also shipped in huge quantities to the Normandy beachhead – by the end of August 181,000 tons of fuel had been delivered to the British alone by this means.

From Normandy, petrol pipelines were linked up and extended to provide a through route from Cherbourg and Port-en-Bessin to Rouen. After 3 October, piped petrol was pumped into storage tanks at Darnetal, north of the Seine just outside Rouen.

With Ostend in Belgium in Allied hands, by 20 September tankers could dock there and discharge fuel directly ashore.

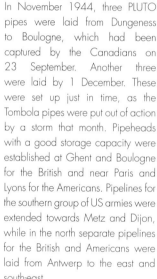

In November 1944, three PLUTO pipes were laid from Dungeness to Boulogne, which had been captured by the Canadians on 23 September. Another three were laid by 1 December. These were set up just in time, as the Tombola pipes were put out of action by a storm that month. Pipeheads with a good storage capacity were established at Ghent and Boulogne for the British and near Paris and Lyons for the Americans. Pipelines for the southern group of US armies were extended towards Metz and Dijon, while in the north separate pipelines for the British and Americans were laid from Antwerp to the east and south-east.

The appetite for fuel of mechanized armies supported by air forces is brought home when one considers that of the three and a half million tons of supplies discharged at ports in France and Belgium in April 1945 alone, including ammunition, replacement tanks and vehicles of all kinds, railway engines and trucks, some 900,000 tons was bulk petrol. There were eventually 11 PLUTO pipes operating, pumping an average of 3,100 tons of fuel a day during March and April 1945; on the last day of the campaign 3,500 tons were delivered. PLUTO had played a major part in supplying what the French called *"le sang rouge de la guerre"* ("the red blood of war").

LEFT: The Pipeline Under the Ocean being reeled out over stern rollers from HMS *Sancroft* in June 1944.

ABOVE: A Conundrum ready to be towed across the Channel.

◼41 The Jeep

The vehicle's official title was the MB 4x4 Truck, but everyone called it a Jeep, and everyone wanted one. Before the Second World War ended, American automobile manufacturers, primarily the Ford Motor Company and Willys-Overland, had made 640,000 Jeeps.

Although the US Army had tried to standardize its family of motor vehicles into six different size classes in 1939, the field exercises of 1940 revealed a requirement for a small dual-drive wheeled vehicle that could carry a driver and three passengers in all sorts of terrain. The final model was powered by a four-cylinder inline engine of 60 hp and was capable of carrying 550 kg (1,200 lbs). Pulling a trailer added to its cargo capacity. It also had to have a removable canvas roof and side panels on a metal frame to deal with bad weather.

The War Department's request for a prototype went to 135 companies with a requirement to propose a design in 49 days. Only the American Bantam Car Company responded, submitting a design by Karl Probst, who drew up plans for the vehicle in two days. It was earlier design work by two Army officers for Bantam that made this response possible.

Because the American Bantam Car Company did not have the plant capacity or workforce to make the new vehicle, the Jeep contract went to Ford and Willys using the Probst-American Bantam Car design under a royalties agreement.

The unloaded vehicle weighed 1,090 kg (2,400 lbs), which meant it could be pushed and pulled by soldiers if necessary. Its four-cylinder engine, 60 hp motor allowed it to creep up steep inclines, yet it could speed along good roads at 89 kph (55 mph). Its range was 450 kilometres (280 miles). It could be adapted to carry radios and stretchers, as well as a mount for a .30-calibre or a .50-calibre machine gun for combat zone missions. It could even pull light anti-tank guns and small howitzers.

Stuck with the name "Jeep" – whose origin is uncertain, but popular theories are that it came from "GP" meaning "general purpose", or was derived from the go-anywhere character Eugene the Jeep in *Popeye* cartoons – in various models and modes the vehicle became common in every Allied army, or was duplicated in some variant, as in the Red Army. American divisions normally rated around 1,350 service support motor vehicles, and of these, 612 would have been Jeeps. Every infantry company had one Jeep and trailer; enterprising units found more than one. Since seven out of every ten GIs came from families that had a car, a truck or a tractor, maintenance and minor repairs could be performed at the unit level. The simplicity of the Jeep's motor made this possible. It's utility in rough terrain made it popular in the Second World War, a popularity that explains the presence of Jeeps in a variety of models all over the world, even today.

ABOVE: A US solider looks over the destroyed city of Saint-Lô from his Jeep.

RIGHT: Finished Jeeps stand in rows having been mass-produced for the Allied invasion of Nazi-Europe.

42 The Green Beret

On the evening of 4 June 1940, Lieutenant Colonel Dudley Clarke, a military assistant to Sir John Dill, Chief of the Imperial General Staff (CIGS), was walking back from the War Office to his flat. At 14.23 hours that afternoon the Admiralty had signalled the end of Operation Dynamo, the evacuation from Dunkirk. The great bulk of the British Expeditionary Force (BEF) had been extracted from France and Flanders, but the outlook was grim.

In 49 days the Germans had occupied Denmark, Norway, Holland and Belgium. France was on the verge of collapse and the Channel ports were in the hands of the enemy. Clarke asked himself if there was any way the British army could strike back, and recalled how, some 40 years earlier, Boer commandos in South Africa, defeated in conventional battles, had harried huge numbers of British troops. He committed his ideas to paper and gave this to his boss, who presented it to the Prime Minister, Winston Churchill. Two days later, Dill told Clarke that his Commando scheme was approved and he was to mount a raid across the Channel at the earliest possible moment.

Even before the first raid, the question arose of what this force should be called. Someone in the War Office had already started calling them Special Service Battalions, either forgetting or ignoring the fact that the initials SS stood for the infamous Nazi *Schutzstaffel*. The CIGS decreed that the new force would be known as Commandos, although the brigades retained the name Special Service until late in 1944.

To begin with all Commandos wore their own regimental head-dress and badge, but in May 1942, Admiral Mountbatten, then Chief of Combined Operations, under whose command the Commandos came, wrote to the Under Secretary of State for War:

I have received a request from the Commander of the Special Service Brigade that the Brigade should be allowed to wear a distinctive form of head-dress.
2. Approval is therefore requested for them to wear a green beret similar in design to the maroon beret worn by the Airborne Division and on which officers and men would wear the badge of their own regiment.
3. I have been much struck by the intense desire on the part of all officers and men with whom I have spoken to have a distinctive form of head-dress and consider that it would make the greatest difference to esprit-de-corps.
4. I have discussed this matter personally with the Adjutant General before forwarding this official request.

The new beret was not issued until October 1942, and not all men were as keen to wear it as Mountbatten had implied: the colour was thought effeminate. But "feelings soon changed and it was not long before the practical and prestigious value of the green beret outweighed any colour prejudice" (*The Light Blue Lanyard: 50 Years with 40 Commando Royal Marines*, Major J C Beadle, Square One Publication, 1992). The green beret was worn with pride in action and on parade, in preference to any other head-dress. Royal Marines and Army Commandos wear it to this day.

FAR LEFT: A Commando with a silenced Sten and wearing a Denison Smock.

ABOVE & LEFT A British Royal Marines Commando beret featuring a metal Royal Marines cap insignia.

■43 The Panzerfaust

The Panzerfaust ("armour fist") was a German shoulder-launched anti-tank weapon. It was the second generation of its type, the first being the Panzerschreck. The Americans had been first to produce a shoulder-launched anti-tank rocket fired from a 60-mm (2.36-in) tube: the Bazooka. Although a pre-war idea, it was not effective until the invention of the shaped or hollow charge, which could defeat armour. The principle was to mould the explosive round a cone, which increased its power by up to 15 times.

Until then, armour-piercing weapons relied solely on firing a projectile made of very hard steel, which "drilled" its way through the armour by virtue of its kinetic energy; some anti-armour weapons rely on this characteristic to this day. To produce the necessary muzzle velocity requires a large and powerful gun, which cannot be carried around by an infantry soldier. As the war progressed and tanks with heavier armour appeared on the battlefield, anti-tank guns became correspondingly bigger. The British army, for example, developed from the useless Boyes anti-tank rifle and 25-mm Hotchkiss in 1939 to the very effective 17-pounder in 1943. Anti-tank guns had to be towed or fitted in vehicles, and were difficult to conceal because of the dust and flame of their muzzle blast.

The hollow charge changed this. It works by projecting a stream of super-hot molten metal through the armour, which sprays the interior of the vehicle, killing the crew and setting fire to ammunition and fuel. This often causes a massive explosion, on occasions big enough to blow the turret off a tank. A hollow charge does not have to be especially large to achieve a "kill" against an armoured vehicle. With the addition of an aerodynamic nose cone, it can be fixed to a rocket, and this, with the launcher, is light enough to be carried by an infantry soldier.

The American Bazooka was sent in considerable numbers to Russia, where several fell into German hands. The Germans copied it and produced the Panzerschreck, which fired an electrically-ignited 88-mm rocket grenade. It was operated by two men, one to carry and fire it, the other to carry spare rockets and load the tube. It had a range of 135 metres (150 yards), and could penetrate 21cm (8.25in) of armour. The tube could be reloaded, and, like a Bazooka, fired as often as there were rockets available.

The Panzerfaust also fired a hollow-charge bomb, but from a disposable tube. It was light, and could be carried and fired by one man. It first appeared in late 1942, had a range of up to 90 metres (100 yards), and could penetrate 19.8 cm (7.8 in) of armour. It was cheap, and over six million were manufactured during the war. It was widely used by the German army, and, towards the end of the war, by the *Volkssturm*.

In built-up areas and thick country such as the Normandy Bocage, it was extremely effective. Small bodies of infantry could hide in ambush and, having allowed a tank to pass them, could fire a Panzerfaust into the side or rear of the tank, where the armour was usually thinner. For this reason the Panzerfaust was feared by Allied tank crews, especially when fighting in towns or villages, around agricultural buildings, and in terrain consisting of woods and thick hedgerows.

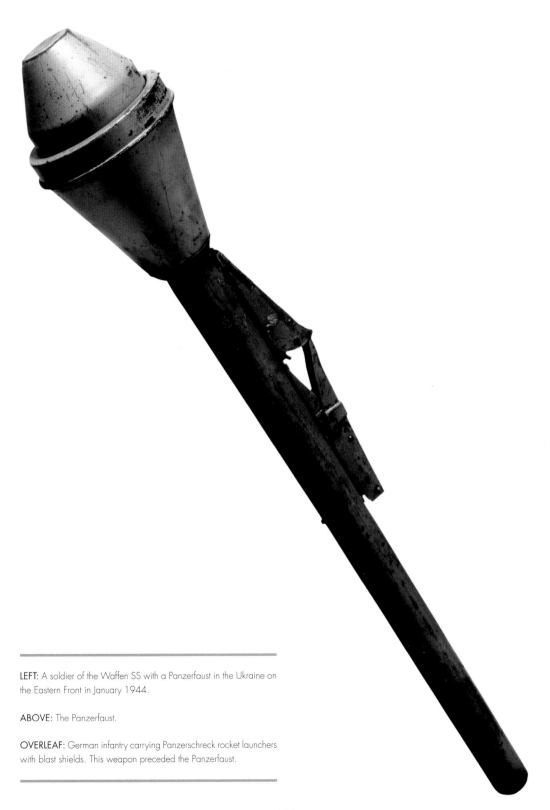

LEFT: A soldier of the Waffen SS with a Panzerfaust in the Ukraine on the Eastern Front in January 1944.

ABOVE: The Panzerfaust.

OVERLEAF: German infantry carrying Panzerschreck rocket launchers with blast shields. This weapon preceded the Panzerfaust.